Training Aids

IN THEORY AND PRACTICE

Training Aids

IN THEORY AND PRACTICE

Elwyn Hartley Edwards

J A ALLEN
London

British Library Cataloguing in Publication Data
Hartley, Edwards, Elwyn 1927—
    Training Aids
    1. Livestock: Horses. Training
    I. Title
    636.1083

ISBN 0-85131-528-3

Reprinted 1994

First published in Great Britain in 1990 by
J. A. Allen & Company Limited
1 Lower Grosvenor Place
London SW1W 0EL

Design and book production Bill Ireson
Photoset by Waveney Typesetters, Norwich
Printed by Longdunn Press, Bristol

This book is for those who keep an open mind and who cultivate the ultimate quality of the horseman or woman, that of humility

Contents

List of Illustrations

Introduction

It seems incumbent upon an author presenting a book under the title carried by this one to attempt a definition of the words 'training aids'. Just what is a training aid, in what respects does it differ from an artificial aid and at what point does it become a gadget?

The use and nature of restraining and corrective aids, to which a short section is devoted, is implicit in the wording and presents no problem. That is not so in the wider field of training equipment. Indeed, one is bound to conclude that there is a deal of muddled, or at least illogical, thinking about the whole subject.

As an example, we have the long-standing definitions of 'natural' and 'artificial' aids that are repeated continually in an assortment of training manuals and are, indeed, enshrined in the manual of the 'official' British governing body, the British Horse Society, and its affiliated association, the Pony Club.

The 'natural' aids, we are told, are those concerned with the limbs, body-weight and voice. The 'artificial' ones are defined as being whips and spurs. It is an understandable simplification but it is, none the less, incomplete and even illogical. If whip and spur, reinforcing the leg aids, are artificial, then so are a lot of other items – in particular, the drop-noseband, which, by forcibly closing the mouth, enhances the effect of the hand.

The drop-noseband is universally accepted as being integral to the snaffle bridle. Used improperly, or constructed incorrectly, however, its potential to do harm is very great – a matter discussed in the preceding book of this trilogy, *Bitting: In Theory and Practice*, where nosebands are studied as auxiliaries to the bit and, it follows, also to the hand.

The drop-noseband is, none the less, accepted as a legitimate piece of equipment and that is quite reasonable as long as its fitting and subsequent action are understood clearly by those employing it. I cannot imagine that it would ever be described as a 'gadget', even though there are other items of equipment, no more coercive in their action, that are condemned by being labelled as such.

Gadget is one of those unfortunate words that have taken on a different meaning through common, if incorrect, usage, rather like 'gay', 'queer' and so on. It is a pity that its use in the equestrian context has come to be associated with articles considered to be less than acceptable and even to be associated with undesirably forceful methods, or, at best, gimmickry.

The *Oxford English Dictionary* defines this innocent enough word as 'a small tool or piece of mechanism', suggesting that the origin is a nautical one. The more general definition is given as 'an accessory or adjunct, especially of a trivial character'. That is nearer the mark as far as the word's use in equestrian terminology goes. 'Trivial' may not be appropriate to many of the articles used in schooling the horse, but 'accessory' and 'adjunct' certainly are. Moreover, the words carry no overtones of coercion.

The FEI (Fédération Equestre Internationale), the world governing body for equestrian sports, just holds back from challenging the authority of the *OED*, but by implication and/or exclusion it indicates in its rules those items considered to be, in the popular sense, within the gadget category.

A paragraph (presently No. 53) in the BHS Dressage Group booklet *Dressage Rules and Official Dressage Judges* is headed 'Gadgets'. It details equipment that *is* permissible in affiliated competitions or when warming up for such competitions. It can be assumed, therefore, that those items that are *not* permitted, whether detailed or not, are considered as gadgetry and do not find approval. In fact, preceding paragraphs specify such forbidden articles.

Inevitably, there are some inconsistencies and illogicalities in the rulings of this august body – it is, for instance, permitted to use a metal curb chain and, presumably to prevent chafing, to cover this with a rubber or leather guard, but, as the rule is written, the softer leather curb, or one made from elastic, is not allowed. (Perhaps this is a 'deliberate mistake', made to remind us that the status of 'official body' is no more synonymous with infallibility than any other of our human institutions.) It is, indeed, obligatory for governing bodies to formulate rules for the conduct of their sports and it is not the purpose of this book to contest their validity (which does not, I hope, preclude the occasional irreverent, but otherwise friendly, dig).

In this book the training aids are looked upon as 'auxiliaries and adjuncts', intended to help the rider in obtaining a carriage or outline or to improve this; or it may be a device designed to remedy or correct a particular failing in the horse's conformation, action or behaviour.

These aids are discussed in terms of their use, action and objective, without being accorded specific approval or otherwise. It is up to the reader to make up his or her own mind about the validity of these items – but to do so with a sound understanding of the principles and actions involved, and that is something the book seeks to clarify.

It is often said that 'gadgets are for experts and experts don't use them', which is quite untrue. Experts all over the world do use them, and if only for that reason we lesser folk should understand what is used and why.

There is also another, more tolerant saying – 'One man's gadget is another man's system.' And that is the last time the degraded noun will appear in this text.

(The action of the straightforward standing and running martingales and the various types of noseband in relation to the bit are discussed in detail in the second book of this trilogy, *Bitting: In Theory and Practice.*)

1: Early Training Aids – 'Helps and Corrections'

Ever since 'Man, encompassed by the elements which conspired to destroy him, by beasts faster and stronger than himself', perceived that he 'would have been a slave had not the horse made him a king', the human race has been concerned to bend the horse to its purpose, to control and channel the horse's enormous physical power and to impose human ideals of perfection upon it.

Ancient Horsemen

The early Egyptians used a pretty fearsome drop-noseband on their chariot horses in order to keep them in hand, or nearly so, in the heat of battle. (Aeons later, in the nineteenth century, von Oeynhausen of the Austrian cavalry introduced a *Reithalter* (a riding halter or noseband) that varied very little from the Egyptian pattern. In time, it became the 'German', sometimes 'Hannoverian', drop-noseband, which is almost what we use today.)

The prototype for the famous (some would say infamous) modern balancing rein appears in its essentials on the carved façade of the temple of Rameses III at Medinet Habu.

The Persians used a studded noseband connected to the bit, the forerunner of the cruel-toothed *cerreta* of the fifteenth-century Spanish *gineta* horseman. (To ride *à la gineta* was to ride short 'in the Turkey fashion' and after the manner of the steppe horsemen.) The *cerreta*, which without doubt compelled the horse to carry its head in an overbent position, produced a result without touching the mouth, but at the expense of a scarred and calloused nose. From it was developed the cavesson, an almost identical article to the modern lungeing cavesson, from which the Renaissance horsemen progressed to the curb bit.

Far more severe was the *musrole*, a noseband of twisted iron much favoured in the early schools of Naples.

The Renaissance

Classical horsemanship in its early period, under masters like Federico Grisone and his pupil Pignatelli, was, indeed, much concerned to exorcise the 'shrewd toys' and the devils of disobedience to which the wretched horse of the period was deemed to be heir. Seven aids or 'helps' were used by the early *manège* rider supported by numerous 'corrections'. These 'helps' were the voice, tongue, rod or wand, bridle, calves of the legs, stirrups and spurs.

The Renaissance horseman would have found no favour in the modern dressage ring on account of his liberal use of the first help, the voice, and his clicking of the tongue to assist in halts and turns. For 'disorders' he was instructed to rate the horse with 'a terrible voice – "Ah, traitor, ah traitor, turn here, stop there"' and so on. To encourage the horse, a cheerful tone of voice was to be employed – 'Hey, hey', 'Now, now' and suchlike endearments. To praise him, the rider was to utter such 'cloying words' as 'Holla, holla' or 'So boy, so boy'. There were also such instructions as 'Hup, hup', and the less comprehensible *'Derrière, derrière'*, when the horse was required to activate its quarters.

The rod, other than as a means of punishment, was used in turning or circling, when it was tapped on the shoulder or waved alongside the horse's head. To tap the foreleg was a signal to rein back or to raise both legs in a *levade* (the half-rear on quarters deeply engaged under the body). Tapping the croup caused the horse to raise the quarters in *croupade* or to leap, lashing out behind, in the *capriole*. Swishing the whip in the air was the signal to increase pace. The bridle was used, tactfully, to maintain the carriage and prevent the horse from making off under the assault made on it with the rod, while the leg-aids varied in severity in the sequence of legs, stirrup and spur.

'Treading the ring' was another training aid, the horse being schooled on a variety of rings, turns etc., on narrow, hardened tracks made in heavy plough. As an additional support, much use was made of footmen armed with cudgels, spiked rods, hot irons, bundles of burning straw and other coercive instruments, such as an infuriated cat, tied belly upmost to the end of a pole and thrust between the horse's hindlegs 'so as she may scratch and bite him, sometime by the thighs, sometime by the rump and often time by the stones' (testicles). A live hedgehog tied by the foot under the horse's tail was also recommended as, in extremity, was a rope tied round 'the stones' and passing thence to the rider's hand!

The first of the French masters was the gifted Antoine de Pluvinel (1555–1620), a gentleman by birth, and a soldier, diplomat and, at one time, tutor to Louis XIII. He studied under Pignatelli, the 'third man' in the classical progression and the link between the early masters and those of the new enlightenment. The main emphasis in Pluvinel's methods, made clear in his book *Manège du Roy*, is on the humanitarian approach based on an understanding of the horse's physical and mental capabilities, although it did not preclude the use of an assortment of severe bits etc.

Pluvinel condemned the violent methods of his predecessors, relying increasingly on a progression of gymnastic suppling exercises. It was he who was responsible for the introduction of 'the pillars', the indispensable adjunct (training aid) and hallmark of the classical schools to this day. Tied by various lengths of rope to a single pillar, the horse was taught the school circles and some of the movements. At a later date, in Guérinière's* day, the master used the single pillar to teach

---

François Robichon de la Guérinière [1688–1751] was equerry to Louis XIV at the Tuileries. He was the inventor of shoulder-in, the first to use counter-canter and the first to practise the flying change of leg. He is acknowledged as being the greatest single influence on the development of riding. His teachings, expounded in *Ecole de Cavalerie*, became the basis of instruction at Vienna's Spanish Riding School.

shoulder-in, the movement he 'invented'. Tied from the cavesson between two pillars, the horse could be taught the *piaffe, levade, croupade* and *ballotade*. Pluvinel's other 'training aids' were the *chambrière* and the *poinçon*, the former being a short whip with a broad, flat keeper or lash, rather like that used by the Argentine gaucho today. It was used to stimulate the horse from behind. It made a noise when applied but it could scarcely be said to hurt and it certainly could not cut a horse.

The *poinçon* was a wooden handle fitted with an iron point at its end. Applied to the croup it caused the horse to kick up his heels (not unreasonably one might think)!

Fifty years later, the sole British master, William Cavendish, Duke of Newcastle, was extending equestrian practice and continuing the encouragement of a humane approach. Newcastle was among the most incompetent of cavalry commanders – he was largely responsible for the defeat of his own side, the Royalists, at Marston Moor – but he ranks, none the less, as one of the great masters of equitation.

It was he who developed the directional use of rein on either side of the horse, and who appreciated the use of the rider's body-weight as an aid. He also invented the running rein, which was usually passed through the side rings of the cavesson. For this device, and perhaps unfairly, he has been castigated by later generations. Possibly, Newcastle relied too much on his brainchild but, none the less, it was copied, improved and much employed by some of the greatest European horsemen in the succeeding centuries, notably those of the German school.

Louis Seeger, a favourite pupil of the famous Max von Weyrother at the Spanish Riding School where von Weyrother was Chief Rider from 1825 until his death in 1833, produced his own version of the rein, based on Weyrother's pattern. Seeger's pupil was Gustav Steinbrecht, acknowledged as the architect of the German system, and an avowed admirer of Newcastle. In fact, it was the German school that most likely ensured the survival of the running rein and it is probable that the best exponents of its use today are the German showjumpers.

Training aids employed when schooling in hand, either on the lunge or in long reins, were in use in the sixteenth century, when items like side reins, martingales and ambling harness

Gibson's Patent Action Developer which employed very strong
elastic cords. It was claimed that the horse's upward action would be
increased by 38–41 cm (15–18 in) by using this developing harness

The modern harness-racer's pacing hobbles used to encourage the
pacing gait. A very similar piece of equipment was used to confirm
the ambling gait in the sixteenth century. (The amble is a slow,
comfortable version of the pacing gait.)

were commonplace enough. Horses were taught to amble in hobbles (very similar to the harness-racing pacer's hobbles today), ropes being fastened to hobbles attaching near-fore to near-hind and off-fore to off-hind, so as to encourage the lateral gait. Wooden weights or balls were also strapped to the heels in order to make a horse pick its feet up. This device was not unknown to Xenophon (430–355 BC) and much the same thing is to be seen on American gaited horses of the present day.

Interestingly, action developers for harness horses and, indeed, ridden ones too, were still in use between the wars in Britain. The most famous were the Gibson patterns employing elastic cords. They were the invention of George Gibson MRCVS of Oakham, a noted horseman whose practice remains in the family and is still at Oakham.

The training aids of the twentieth century are less numerous than in the past, a reflection, one hopes, of better techniques and a greater understanding of riding theory, and they are certainly not brutal in nature. Like any other piece of equipment, however, they become unacceptable when used unacceptably.

(Horses pace when their legs are used in alternative lateral pairs – i.e. left fore and hind and then right fore and hind. The amble is a slower and more comfortable version of the pacing gait.)

2: Breaking and Schooling Tackle

Submission and the obedience training of the young horse begin almost as soon as it is born and by the time it is nine days old it should be possible for the foal to be held and handled. A little later it will be haltered and will learn to lead in hand.

Leading in hand from both sides, with the trainer positioning himself at the horse's shoulder and not advancing beyond that point, is the basis for future work on the lunge and long reins and is the horse's first lesson in the essential requirement of free forward movement.

Preparatory to beginning the education of the young horse through exercises on the lunge, it is essential that it should have learnt to walk and trot on a lead rein in hand. This can be taught quite easily by a trainer standing at the horse's shoulder, carrying a long schooling or dressage whip in his outside hand (i.e. left hand if leading from the near side) and holding the lead rein, attached to the central ring of a cavesson, in his inside hand about 25 cm (10 in) from the point of attachment. The slack of the rein is taken across the trainer's body to the outside hand. Keeping his position, the trainer gives the command 'walk-on' or 'walk-march' or indeed any other combination of words. As long as the same command is always used, the horse will associate it with the movement required.

At the same time as the command is given, the trainer, using the whip behind his back, taps the animal's flank and steps forward resolutely. It helps, of course, if an assistant is available to walk up behind and encourage the horse's movement to the front.

Galvayne's Harness

There is another aid that can be used to teach horses to walk and trot in hand. It is called Galvayne's harness and it is also a useful piece of equipment with which to load a horse into a trailer or box, particularly if one is single-handed.

In its simple form it is nothing more than a loop of soft rope passed round the quarters and then up towards the wither. It can be kept in place by a breast rope or any arrangement that will support the rope and prevent it from dropping to the ground. The ends of the rope continue forward and are passed through the side dees of a headcollar or the rear dees of a schooling cavesson in the case of a youngster, or, if the horse is wearing a bridle, through the bit rings. A quick pull on the rope ends at the front results in the loop tightening on the animal's rear and causes understandable puzzlement in the equine mind, as the horse has difficulty in associating the handler at its front end with the persuasion it is experiencing from the rear. In a very short space of time, indeed, the horse moves forward easily and willingly.

A more persuasive effect can be obtained by passing the rope under the dock or even by knotting the rope round that part. This method effectively quashes resistance and ensures immediate compliance with the request to move forward.

The illustrations of Galvayne's harness in his book *The Horse* differ a little from the variation I have described (there are indeed any number of variants to his basic equipment) but the effect is basically the same. Galvayne also used this simple piece of equipment for yet another purpose – as an effective way in which to frustrate the horse that continually pulls back against the headcollar when tied up. In this instance, the horse will receive the pull of the harness on its tail or round its quarters as a result of throwing its own weight backwards. There is no pull on the headcollar, which is what the horse expected, nothing has broken and, instead of becoming free, the horse has inflicted some unexpected discomfort on itself. The psychological effect is considerable and the thinking behind it sound. (It would, of course, be advisable for the handler to remain within easy reach of the stable when the harness was being worn in case of an accident caused by panic.) The principle of a psychological force being applied by a mechanical one activated by the horse itself, was very much a part of the tradition of horse-

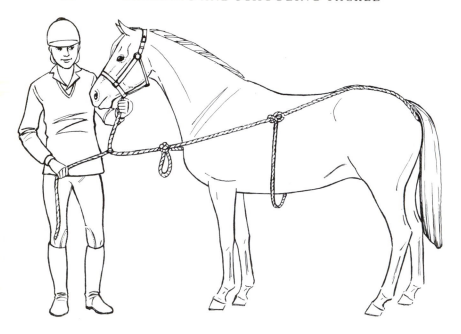

Two variations of Galvayne's leading harness

taming to which Galvayne belonged. The use of the tail, in particular, was integral to the system, as were the hobbles, ropes and surcingles that were part of the horse-tamer's stock-in-trade.

Most of the famous horse-tamers were of American or Australian origin and some of them, like Solomon Rarey and Galvayne himself, found fame in Europe after making tours demonstrating their skill with 'uncontrollable' horses. Sydney Galvayne, who, like most of his peers, assumed the courtesy title of 'Professor', came to Britain from America in 1884, appearing before Queen Victoria at Balmoral in 1887 to demonstrate his 'new, humane and scientific system'. His early career, however, is obscure.

He was an Australian certainly, but his real name was Osborn, which he changed to Galvayne on his arrival in England. He may possibly have done so because of disputes between himself and his former employer in America, 'Professor' Sample. It has been suggested that Galvayne's system was really the work of Sample who may also have been the author of the celebrated system of aging horses by looking at their teeth, a system we still employ today. Galvayne claimed this as his own, publishing the details in his book *Horse Dentition* and assuring himself a certain immortality through Galvayne's groove, the mark that appears at the top of the upper corner incisor at nine years or thereabouts. At ten years the groove is about 6mm (¼ in) long and it advances down the tooth at the rate of about 3mm (⅛ in) each year. At fifteen years it has reached halfway and it touches the bottom at about twenty years.

In addition to 'the groove', Sydney Galvayne was responsible for the introduction of a new verb to the equestrian vocabulary, 'to galvayne'. Galvayning was a means of subjugating the vicious horses with which the nineteenth century seems to have abounded. It involved the fixing of an adjustable connecting strap between the headcollar ring and the horse's tail, the body, in consequence, being bent in a shallow U-shape. The horse was immediately prevented from violent action, the only movement open to it being the execution of a small circle. There is no doubt that the tail was critical in the subjugation of the horse by

Galvayning – a means of
subjugating the awkward
customer

this method, and it was certainly important in the horse-tamer's philosophy. After even a short time in this uncomfortable position, the horse could be released and, on all the evidence available (which is copious), would then behave quite docilely and allow itself to be handled, saddled and bridled etc. Once more, this is an example of a psychological force being exerted by a mechanical action that, although uncomfortable, causes no actual hurt other, perhaps, than to the horse's dignity, and it demonstrates indisputably the trainer's authority.

Another noted horseman, Major Barrowcliff-Ellis, an officer of the Indian Army in the days of the Raj, attributed the Galvayne system, which he practised extensively in the breaking of remounts, to a German named Lichtwark who had settled in Australia in 1865. Whatever the truth of it, and in its essentials it could well be that some parts of the Galvayne system were practised by the ancient horse-peoples long before Europeans set foot in either America or Australia, it was through Galvayne that it obtained recognition. Sydney Galvayne was, without doubt, a horseman of exceptional talent; he was also no mean veterinarian as well as being a considerable authority on equine dentition. He lectured at the Royal Veterinary College, was the author of some half-dozen books, and during the South African War he was appointed Director of Breaking to the Imperial Army! (Galvayne's 'third hand' method, termed the 'blob stick' by Barrowcliff-Ellis, is described in Chapter 12, which deals with means of restraint and correction.)

The methods of the old horse-tamers are still known and practised in America and Australia and less 'scientifically', and possibly less humanely, in the steppe countries that were the home of the first horse-peoples. These methods are not unknown in Europe, but may not have much relevance to modern systems. They are worthy of study by the serious student, however, for they represent the output of men who were horsemen in ways not open to us and almost beyond our understanding.

Lungeing

The practice of lungeing forms the larger part of the young horse's primary education. It is carried out in the animal's third year and it constitutes the preparation of the horse, both physically and mentally, for the later work under saddle. (There is an increasing tendency, particularly in Europe, to begin schooling at two years. This is to be deplored for it subjects the immature frame to stresses that it is unable to sustain. As a result, too many horses become unsound in their early years and their useful working life is shortened significantly as a result. Thoroughbred race horses, bred for early maturity, are, for economic reasons, broken and raced as two year olds. They are produced and managed skilfully, but the wastage that never the less occurs as a result of unsoundness is a telling argument against the practice.)

The objectives to be achieved by lungeing and the benefits that accrue from the exercises being performed well under the care of a skilled handler are these:

1   It promotes muscular development, without allowing this to form in opposition to the weight of the rider. Done skilfully, this occurs equally on both sides of the body.
2   The horse is made supple through the equal stretching and

contraction of the dorsal, neck and abdominal muscles on each side.

3   There is encouragement to extend and lower the head, to round the back, and to work with increased engagement of the hindlegs. (On the circle the inside hindleg will be compelled to engage more actively under the body.)

4   As a result of greater and more supple muscular development, there is an increase in the flexion of the joints.

5   The overall balance is improved, largely because of increased hock engagement, and the gaits become increasingly refined in terms of cadence, rhythm and tempo.

Mentally, the horse learns to work in a state of calm. He learns obedience to the voice and develops and accepts habitual discipline. Finally, he acquires the quality of *forward movement*, which is as much a manifestation of a mental outlook as a physical response.

(Lungeing is also a useful way in which to exercise an over-fresh horse before getting into the saddle or to work one that, for one reason or another, cannot be ridden. Lungeing a ridden horse that is well schooled in the exercise is also valuable in the training of the rider and the improvement of the seat position.)

Lunge Equipment

Boots and Cavesson

Boots on all four legs are essential to protect the legs from the blows that can occur when young horses are still largely uncoordinated in their movements. However, the boots need to be substantial enough to give *full* protection. Little, light, brushing-type boots are worse than useless for they promote a sense of false security in the trainer.

Of prime importance to the execution of the exercise is the **cavesson**. This is a powerful means of control and needs to be handled with care. It must fit perfectly if it is to be effective and it must provide all the points of attachment that are necessary.

One or two modern cavessons are well designed and constructed, but most of them fall below that fundamentally acceptable standard and nearly all perpetuate the anachronism

The horse in full lungeing gear: cavesson, roller, side-reins, crupper
and protective boots

Two types of lunge cavesson. The heavier one (*left*) is fitted with side rings which are so positioned as to be of little practical use. The light cavesson (*right*) is a better pattern but would benefit from the addition of rings behind the cheek pieces to which side reins could be attached

of a nose-plate fitted with three rings. The two outer rings were originally (well over 400 years ago) placed further to the rear where they projected outwards, virtually at right angles. It was, therefore, quite possible to fit a rein to them and to ride from the cavesson. (The horses drawing *fiacre*-type vehicles seen plying for hire in Mediterranean countries today are frequently driven from just such a cavesson.)

The present-day three-ring cavessons are still quite suitable for their original intended purpose; that is, to attach the horse between two training pillars by the outside rings, but otherwise these two rings are superfluous. There may be one or two people in faraway places who lunge from the inside ring in accordance with some arcane theory of their own. The rest of us lunge from the centre ring, which is logical as it gives greater control, is more convenient and allows greater finesse in the handling of the lunge rein. One can, of course, ride off the cavesson preparatory to transferring the control to the bit rein but *not* from the side-rings, which are placed too far forward for that to be any sort of option.

For practical purposes, even if the cavesson still retains the superfluous outer rings, two further dees need to be sewn to the nosepiece, one on each side, to provide an anchorage for a bit to be suspended from them. In course of time, side reins can be fitted without the necessity of putting on a bridle under the cavesson. Two more rings, fitted above the bit dees, allow for the side reins to be fastened directly to the cavesson, which one might wish to do in the early stages, prior to putting the reins to the bit. It is also possible to ride from these rings.

A jowl strap is essential, to prevent the cavesson being pulled round so that the cheekpiece slides up against the eye. However, it must be positioned properly if it is to achieve this purpose – and most of them are not. Do not buy a cavesson unless you have had the opportunity to fit it to the horse.

To complete the cavesson one needs a browband, which will help to keep the head strap in place and also accustoms the horse to wearing one. Young horses are often apprehensive about their ears being pulled through pieces of leather and to avoid an unnecessary disagreement it is a good idea to have a browband made with studs so that the ends can be passed under and round the headpiece, being then turned back and secured to the stud. This avoids the difficulty of pulling the cavesson on over the ears. Obviously, the cavesson has to fit very snugly if it is to stay in place and the nose ring must be set on a swivel to allow for the movement of the rein.

Lunge rein
The best lunge reins are made from tubular web, which is soft, strong and less likely to burn should it be pulled through an ungloved hand (moral – always wear gloves). Lunge reins do not need to be too heavy; 2·5-cm (1 in) width is quite sufficient and 10·5 m (35 ft) is a practical length. The fastening to the cavesson ring can be made with a strap and buckle set on a swivel or, more satisfactorily, with a *very reliable* pattern of snap-hook similarly mounted. Nylon lunge reins are strong and cheaper than webbing, but do not have sufficient substance to provide the ideal contact weight with the nose. A lunge rein, or a pair of

them, is also a useful adjunct to the trailer or horse-box in the absence of Galvayne's harness. (See Chapter 14.)

The roller
A roller provides points of attachment for side reins etc. and for a crupper. It also allows for the long reins to be passed through dees on either side of the body. It is, therefore, the centrepiece of the schooling tackle, a sort of control console. There is also a further purpose: working the horse in a roller accustoms the animal to tension round its barrel and is a commonsense preparation for the saddle and girth. (It can, indeed, be left in place in the stable for short periods of time in order to familiarise the horse with the feel of the girth around its body.)

Of whatever material it is made, the body roller is best constructed in two parts so that it can be adjusted precisely on both sides. Three large rings, spaced equally along the front edge of each side, so that the lowest one is about half-way down the horse's body, provide attachment points for side reins, and the centre one can also be used for long reins. Otherwise, large fixed rings can be sewn below the bottom of the panels to hold the long reins. This, indeed, is probably the best method. A further ring, capable of adjustment, is fitted between the panels on the front edge, and a ring for a crupper on the rear edge. Finally, a large ring is sewn to the centre of the belly girth between the forelegs in case it should be needed for some form of martingale.

It has become something of an article of faith to insist upon a breast girth being worn with a body roller. The argument for using one is that it eliminates the necessity to girth the roller tightly. For myself, I consider it an unnecessary encumbrance. I would certainly use a breast girth on a stable roller, where it has a purpose, but I see no reason why a schooling roller, in which, like the saddle, the horse is required to work, cannot be girthed firmly enough to keep it in place. In any case, if it is going to slip it will slip *forwards*, because the horse is shaped that way. If it shifts backwards the horse is hardly likely to be well enough made ever to develop into a satisfactory riding horse.

When the roller does slip it is usually because it is not properly made, particularly in respect of the pads, and/or it has

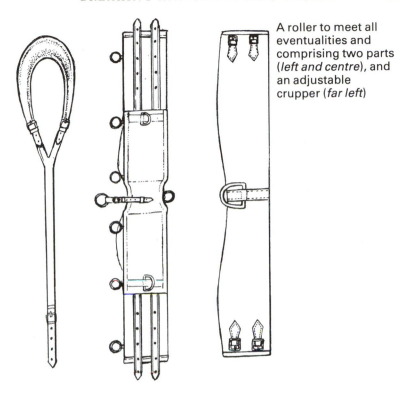

A roller to meet all eventualities and comprising two parts (*left and centre*), and an adjustable crupper (*far left*)

been put on incorrectly. The roller pads, well shaped to ensure that no pressure is put on the spine, should fit like a saddle, lying behind the trapezius muscle and not interfering with the scapula. The belly girth must lie in the sternum curve, (the indentation behind the chest), which we can think of in this context as being the equivalent of the human waist. The roller will then incline a little to the rear of the vertical, the line sloping a little forward from the pads to the sternum. If the belly girth is shaped back at its front edge, there will be no chance of it chafing behind the elbows.

A less ring-bestrewn type of roller, favoured by many trainers, has buckles set on the pads at an angle so that the side reins can cross over the wither. In some instances, there is an advantage in this method in securing a steady head-carriage. (I have, indeed, known horsemen, and very educated ones at that, reverse their reins in this fashion when schooling from the saddle. They did so as a corrective measure and only for short periods.) My own preference is for a roller that allows a variation in the position of the side reins, so that if necessary I can use them at a lower position, moving them upwards and closer to the position taken by the rider's hands, as and when I think appropriate.

The cross-over rein adjustment does not allow for this flexibility but that is not to say it is less effective.

The Crupper

There was a time when I set my face against the use of a crupper on the grounds that it might encourage a hollowing of the back. Of course, it could do just that if it was adjusted so tightly as to cause discomfort, but fitted properly, more loose than tight, it has a notable effect upon the overall carriage, encouraging the horse to use its loins, without exerting anything but the lightest tension on the dock. Used in conjunction with the side reins, it does 'bring the horse together' and this is achieved without the side reins being tight. (In its emphasis on the use of the tail and dock, the effect of the crupper seems to reinforce the horse-lore of the old tamers and of the ancient horse-peoples from whom it is derived.)

A further advantage is that it teaches the horse to accept what might be called handling-by-equipment-contact. Initially, most young horses will hump, clamping down the tail and stiffening the back against the unfamiliar feel of the crupper under their tail. They may even express their disapproval in a buck or two, but within minutes they will be going quite happily and another lesson in submission has been taught and learnt.

For everyone's sake, the act of fitting the crupper is made easier if there is an adjustment on both sides of the dock. As a guide, it should be possible to insert an upright hand between the crupper's back strap and the back itself.

The very best type of crupper (the sort used by the professional horsemen) has a dock-piece made of leather that is stuffed with linseed. The heat of the body, combined with the usual type of cleaning grease and the linseed, makes the leather soft and pliable. I have, however, seen DIY cruppers made from a length of rubber hose well wrapped in a bandage, that have worked very satisfactorily

Lunge whip
The lunge whip is an extension of the hand. It allows the trainer to maintain a triangle, with himself as the apex, the horse forming the base and the lunge rein and whip making the sides. Heavy, clumsy whips or ones that are too short are of no use at all.

The modern whips, made of nylon and fibreglass, are light, well balanced and fitted with thongs long enough to reach the horse should it be necessary, although the whip is *never* used to hit the horse.

Side reins
No useful purpose is ever served by allowing the horse to circle the trainer with a hollow back, its head in the air, without engagement of the hocks and lacking an increasingly rhythmical stride. Indeed, to continue lungeing in that fashion only consolidates the faults already present in carriage and muscular development.

Side reins are not considered controversial, but whether their proper use is generally appreciated is less certain. Too many people fit them too tightly, so as to *impose* a head carriage. As a result, the nose is likely to be tucked in but almost inevitably this forced position in front leads to lack of engagement behind, minimal hock flexion and a shortened, restricted stride of the forelegs.

Used intelligently, the side rein is the trainer's friend, otherwise its influence is counter-productive and leads to loss of freedom in the action and a faulty muscular development that will positively detract from the potential performance.

In the early training on the lunge, the primary concern is to accustom the horse to circling calmly round the trainer, to either hand, at walk and trot, to obtain obedience to the verbal commands and also to the gestures made with the whip to encourage free movement. Once that has been established, however, and the horse is developing physically, it is time to concentrate on the definition and refinement of the gaits and,

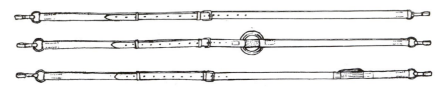

Side reins: (*top*) plain, of the type recommended; (*centre*) inset with a rubber ring; (*below*) elastic inset. Both the latter produce 'give and take' – a largely fallacious philosophy

additionally, on the creation of a balanced outline from which effective movement is made possible.

For that to come about, it is necessary to employ side reins, fitted initially to the cavesson and then to the bit. They will be supported by the whip, pushing the horse forward into the hand, and to a lesser extent by the gentle influence of the crupper. The side reins then act to contain the impulsion created and to produce the required round outline. There must, however, be no suspicion of force. The side reins act in a purely 'suggestive' fashion in terms of carriage. Intelligently used, they should be instrumental in encouraging the horse to reach out to contact the bit, and in skilled hands they will be integral to the process of 'making the mouth' – an art that today, alas, is insufficiently understood or practised. Regarded in that light, the side reins are adjusted to be more loose than tight so that only minimal pressure is felt in the mouth. In a perfect world it is the *weight* of the reins that produces the lightest of contacts with the mouth and induces the easy relaxation of the lower jaw.

My own method is to introduce the side reins when the horse is well able to cross a pole grid actively and in good rhythm on the lunge. I start by walking and then trotting the horse over a single pole laid on the ground and when it crosses the pole quietly I add a second one at a trotting distance to suit its stride. For most horses this will be between 1·3 and 1·5 m (4½–5 ft). Thereafter, I increase the length of the grid by adding more poles until the horse can cope with as many as six.

While crossing the grid the horse is compelled to increase the engagement of the hocks, to round the top-line and to lower and stretch out the head and neck, extending the cervical ligament, which runs from poll to sacrum, on the fulcrum provided by the withers.

At this point I fit the side reins at nearly their full length so that they hang in a definite loop, working the horse in the usual way on the circle. When the horse is well accustomed to the slight pressure on its mouth caused by the weight of the rein, I work it in the reins over the pole grid. *The horse then makes contact with the bit of its own accord* as it stretches forward over the poles and an enormously important lesson has been learnt. The horse is, in fact, seeking out contact with the bit and doing so while in a rounded form.

Thereafter, for the trot work on the circle, the reins can be tightened up gradually, by a hole or two each day, until there is just a slight dip in their centre when the horse is in movement. If they are adjusted any tighter than that, it is likely that the horse

The horse in full lungeing tackle, the side reins exerting the lightest contact

will attempt to evade the contact by retracting its nose and coming 'behind' the bit. In fact, this will still occur occasionally even when the reins are adjusted properly. It happens when the horse is tired and the hindlegs are insufficiently engaged, but that situation is the fault of the trainer not the rein. (Conversely, too tight a rein can cause a hollowing of the back as the horse pushes its head upwards to resist the restriction.)

My own preference is for plain leather side reins fastened, as described, to a body roller made with three dees on each side at varying heights. It is then possible to adjust the height as and when one considers it necessary.

I used to employ elastic- or rubber-inset side reins, being attracted by the possibility of a soft give and take on the mouth. It is, indeed, an appealing thought, but the theory is a fallacious one. The 'give', and more particularly the 'take', of the rein is a positive encouragement to the horse to evade the tension by tucking its nose in and coming away from contact with the bit.

Nor am I impressed by arguments that the inside rein should be adjusted to be shorter than its partner. Again, it sounds logical enough on the surface, but by enforcing a bend (often no more than a twist at the poll) there is every likelihood of the horse either leaning on the inside of the bit or retracting its nose to evade it. The weight, in consequence, is thrown onto the inside shoulder and the quarters are compelled to be carried outwards and away from the track of the forefeet. It is possible and permissible, both in the work from the cavesson and the bit, to make use of a 'running' side rein, an unbroken rein running from one side of the roller to the other and passing either through a ring on the back of the cavesson or through the bit rings. The advantage of such a rein, it is claimed, is that it is less restrictive to the lateral motions of the head.

The reins may also be fitted for short periods while the horse is being ridden under saddle. The purpose in this last instance is to help the rider to establish an acceptable frame within which the horse can be worked to best advantage.

Clearly, in this context there is a possibility of misuse and the danger of the rider becoming reliant upon the side reins to achieve what may appear to be the desired result but is in reality a false carriage. However, in a controlled situation, under the supervision of an instructor, the judicious use of the side reins can be permissible. If, for instance, the rider has difficulty in riding the horse down onto the rein through the purist agencies of back, seat and legs, he or she can be helped to create the required outline and become accustomed to the 'feel' of the horse working within it, by the use of side reins being fitted for ten minutes or so. It can sometimes be difficult, even with a schooled horse, for the pupil to ride the animal into the required outline. In that situation it must be better to put the reins on briefly as a corrective measure than for horse and rider to spend an unprofitable hour achieving nothing more than the confirmation of an ineffectual working carriage.

It is almost impossible to begin collection work without the help of side reins in the initial stages. The early lessons are carried out with the trainer on foot, alongside the horse and facing the rear. He stands at the horse's head holding the lead rein, which is fastened to the centre ring of the cavesson, and with the school whip in his free hand. The horse is positioned along the wall with the side reins adjusted so that the nose is a hand's breadth in front of the vertical and level with the hip joint. The whip is used on the flank, above and below the hock and on the croup so that the horse moves forward in half steps. The rein, used in an upward and backward action, limits the movement forward and leads, when the impulsion is sustained, to collection and a lowering of the quarters. Needless to say, the exercise should only be attempted by an expert, for the whip is applied with just as much finesse as the rein. In both instances it is a matter of 'good hands'.

3: Specialist Tackle

Most trainers will incorporate ideas of their own into the basic lungeing or breaking equipment, but there are one or two specialist tackles that may still be used occasionally and that accentuate some particular feature or vary from the norm in principle.

One of these, popular in Europe and America up to the Second World War, was Blackwell's **dumb jockey** – indeed, there are probably one or two professionals still using it. (It was still being advertised in American catalogues in the mid-1950s.) This was a controversial piece of equipment, against which the establishment inveighed mightily, arguing that it produced a stiff, hollow outline, restricting the action and detracting from forward movement, and going so far as to condemn the tackle as being cruel.

The dumb jockey comprised a roller or 'saddle' to which were fitted a forked pair of gutta-percha arms carrying three adjustment points to which the reins could be attached. The reins either ran from the roller through the bit and back to the forks, or were fitted separately, as a side rein and a top rein, to the forks. Further reins from the forks ran back to the crupper. Very precise adjustments were possible and in the later patterns, exemplified by Blackwell's tackle, use was made of elastic to produce a 'give and take' effect. Mr Blackwell was not, of course, the inventor, he only improved on equipment that was already in existence. The dumb jockey was certainly in use during the seventeenth century, from which time there is pictorial evidence of it at the Spanish School in Vienna.

Of course, it does not find favour today, when we are concerned with the long, low outline (sometimes, perhaps, over-concerned with it to the detriment of a more advanced shape), but the tackle and the outline it produced, which Caprilli had rejected outright in the formulation of his forward system of riding, exactly reflected the thinking of horsemen in Europe well up to the end of the nineteenth century. It was probably used even more extensively in the production of harness horses, to which it may have been more appropriate, and one can

The famous (or infamous) Blackwell Dumb Jockey which is still advertised in American catalogues. Below it is another American speciality, a 'bitting harness' which is not dissimilar to the Carlburg

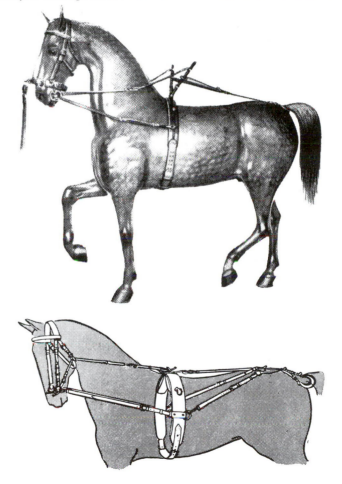

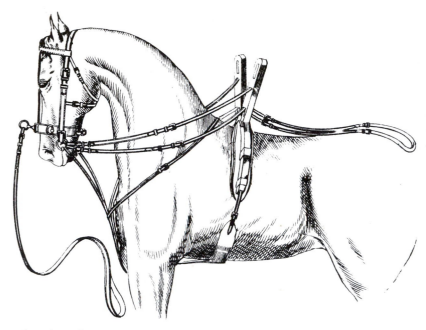

Another nineteenth-century version of the dumb jockey taken from the catalogue of J. Hawkins of Walsall

understand professional dealers employing tackle of this sort in order to produce the finished article more swiftly.

A later variation, which survived the Second World War, was the more sophisticated **Distas** tackle. It was used after the initial lungeing exercises and was popular with the producers of show ponies, whose riders were not strong enough in the leg to obtain a definite result. It is another tackle that is unlikely to find favour today but it is worth studying on account of its great ingenuity and also because it emphasises once more the old principles involving the use of the tail.

The tackle consists of a pretty elaborate bridle employing a Wilson ring bit (i.e. four rings to a single mouthpiece), which causes pressures to be applied to the nose rather than to the mouth. The noseband is made of elastic and is supported by a facepiece. Pulleys are fixed on either side of the headpiece. The

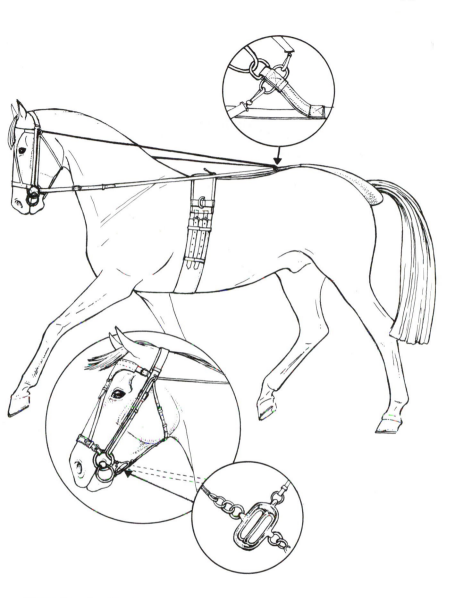

Distas Bending Tackle, a very popular piece of equipment among the professional showing and dealing fraternity up to very recent times. Note the head-raising 'Jodphur' curb lying between the jawbones

bridle is completed by a 'Jodphur' curb, which can be fitted between the jaw bones, and a cord overcheck. The remainder of the tackle is made up of a roller, with a back-strap overlaid with a piece of elastic, fitted with rings, dock crupper and a pair of extended side reins.

The cord overcheck, attached to the chain links of the curb, is passed through and inside the inner rings, thence through the pulleys at the bridle head. The offside cord passes through the smaller of two rings set on the elastic of the back-strap and the overcheck is adjusted by a simple bow on the near side. The curb is prevented from falling out of position by a lip strap fastened to the throat latch of the bridle. The nosepiece of the bridle is fitted fairly tightly and the side reins fastened to the larger ring on the back-strap. The crupper is adjusted with just sufficient tension to raise the tail.

The side reins bring the head to a near vertical position, exerting pressure on the nose for this purpose and the curb and the overcheck act to raise the head to the required level and will prevent the horse from overbending. It was claimed that if correctly fitted, the tackle operated the whole horse, with the loins being brought into play, and that the horse flexed at the poll and not in the lower third of the neck.

It was recommended that the tackle be left on for no more than a few minutes at a time at the outset. Thereafter, the horse was worked loose and finally could be driven in long reins.

If anything belonged to the province of the expert it was this, for it required the most painstaking adjustment and great experience when working the horse. To my certain knowledge, it was still being made for experts and presumably being used by them as late as 1965.

(Overchecks are still used on Hackney harness horses and also, in a simple form, on strong-necked, self-willed children's ponies. Nothing is more frustrating for a small child than to be on a pony who despite all his efforts – hands, legs, stick and often tears – persists in burying its head in the grass to eat. The cure is an overcheck, in basic terms a 'grass string'. It comprises a piece of binder twine tied to each bit ring then passed upwards through the browband loop and back to the saddle dees. Whether it causes all the ills associated with head-

A sophisticated American version of the simple 'grass string' made from binder twine

positioning devices is irrelevant if it stops the little brute's game and allows the child to go for a ride.)

During the same period that these two tackles were in use, a number of 'mouthing' tackles were on sale, designed, of course, to fix the head position. One was an American simplification of the Distas, another, sometimes called the **Carlburg** but which, I suspect, was devised or improved upon in Leicestershire dealing yards, employed a running-rein principle commencing at the wither and passing back to the back-strap of the crupper. Both made much use of elastic insets and expressed the concern of horsemen to obtain a head position and a responsive mouth early in the horse's education and before the ridden work commenced.

Obviously, these curiosities must have worked to a degree, even though they are at variance with the principles we hold today. Their passing from the equestrian scene marks, perhaps, another watershed in the long progression of horse training.

4: Lungeing from the Bit

To lunge an experienced horse from the bit, preparatory to entering the arena at a competition is a convenient practice but has no relevance to schooling. (When it is carried out it is usual for the lunge rein to be fastened to the off-side bit ring on the circle left then taken over the head and passed through the near-side ring to the hand. The opposite fitting is applicable on the circle right.)

There is, however, another method of lungeing from the bit, practised as an extension to the use of the side reins. Its object is to put the horse *in hand*. The side reins taught the horse to make and accept contact with the bit; this method of lungeing from the bit teaches the horse to make and accept contact with the *hand*, which, in this instance, is a different thing altogether as the hand (the 'educated' hand) can yield and resist through a whole range of subtle gradations. At this stage, when the horse is already well established in the lunge exercises, the advantage of the hand being directly in contact with the mouth is that it allows the horse to be *pushed* (by means of the encouraging use of the lunge whip) with far greater effect into contact with the hand.

Some trainers will see the method as being a preparation for the use of long reins, others will regard it as a way of bringing the horse into long-rein training at a more specialist, advanced level than would normally be practised within the general elementary schooling from the ground.

To employ the lunge rein in this advanced manner, use is made of the ring and adjustable strap set on the front of the roller that were referred to earlier. It is also necessary to have a longer rein – 1·8–2·4 m (6–8 ft) longer than the ordinary one and for preference made of light nylon or cotton rope. (At this

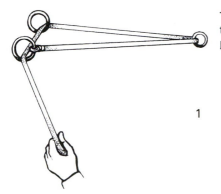

The method of lungeing from
the bit which has the object of
putting the horse *in hand*

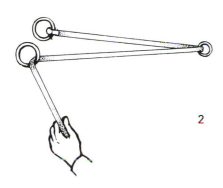

1

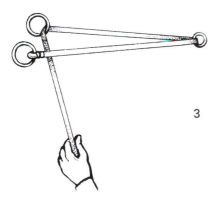

2

3

stage the fact that the rope may burn the hand if pulled through it should not be relevant.) The best type is a tapered cotton plough line with a loop at one end and a light snap hook at the other.

The rein can be used in any one of three positions, Nos 1 and 3 being employed most frequently. The critical factor in the exercise, however, is the length and adjustment of the ring strap. It is, indeed, imperative that this is capable of at least 2·5 or even 5 cm (1–2 in) adjustment each way.

If the strap is too long, the rein 'frames' only the forward part of the neck instead of the whole neck, and that will encourage a 'rubber' neck instead of one like tempered steel. Conversely, too short a strap will be just as bad or even worse, as if the rein is fixed too close to the roller, the neck will 'cave in' in front of the withers, ruining outline, action and carriage.

In Position 1 (shown in the diagram for circle left) the rein operates evenly on both sides of the mouth. For most horses it will not be necessary to make use of the other two positions, which are almost entirely corrective in nature.

Position 2 is a little stronger in its effect upon the inside of the mouth and could be used to induce a little more bend and a greater relaxation of the inside jaw. It should not really be necessary but it is there if needed.

Position 3 helps, *tactfully*, to prevent any inclination on the horse's part to fall inwards.

The whole exercise depends for its success on the skilful handling of the rein, the hand giving light, intermittent squeezes and yielding in accordance with the response made by the horse, and in the trainer's ability to push the horse into contact with his or her hand. The hand is never permitted to force the head and neck to be retracted.

Very recently, a device came onto the market that involves the fixing of a padded weight, of between 1·8–4·8 kg (4–10 lb), being clipped to the bit rings behind the horse's jaw so as to obtain a lowering of the head and neck when the horse is worked on the lunge. If head and neck are thus lowered, it should be possible to obtain a rounded outline and to build up the muscles to accord with it, but only, of course, if there is a *commensurate engagement of the hindlegs under the body,* otherwise the horse is thrown on its forehand and hock engagement becomes minimal.

Of course, the weight produces a corresponding downward pressure on the poll, which is desirable or otherwise according to one's personal opinion. On the other hand, it is unlikely, if fitted snugly, to cause damage to the mouth. The device, albeit blatantly mechanical, is not illogical and has the virtue of simplicity. None the less, it is in the nature of a blunt instrument in comparison with the rapier-like quality of the sophisticated Chambon.

5: The Chambon

Both the **Chambon** and its extension, the **de Gogue**, named after the French cavalry officers who invented them, are simple in concept and are sterling examples of the inescapable Gallic logic that has contributed so greatly to equestrian thinking. Both, indeed, mark another clear division between the change from the backward, dumb-jockey thinking of the nineteenth century, to the forward extension upon which, in later years, collection has been properly based. Since the governing property of muscle is that it can be compressed, or 'collected', in direct ratio to the extent to which it can be stretched or extended – the former being dependent upon the degree of lengthening that can first be obtained – both devices deserve proper attention. Furthermore, by the stretching of the cervical ligament over the fulcrum of the withers, these pieces of equipment encourage the engagement of the quarters, the rounding of the top-line and the inevitable build-up of muscle to correspond with, and, indeed, to command, that outline.

The Chambon and the de Gogue represent basic truths, and both have been unnecessarily complicated and distorted by the convoluted thinking of their self-appointed interpreters. Indeed Messieurs Chambon and de Gogue would be amazed at what has been read into their simple auxiliaries, which do no more than support accepted and proven training methods enshrined forever in the teachings of the latter-day masters like Stein-brecht – '... when both forces of the hindquarters – the propulsive and the carrying power – coupled with elasticity, are fully developed and when the trainer can use and balance the effect of these forces directly ...'.

The Chambon is a schooling device used in conjunction with the lunge exercises, but more particularly when working the

horse loose, when it becomes even more effective as no inward
pressure is exerted from the cavesson ring. In Britain it is not in
general use, being excluded from most training manuals, and its
purpose is not, therefore, sufficiently understood. On the other
hand, the Chambon is employed extensively on the European
mainland where it is often regarded as being as integral to the
work on the lunge as the lunge rein and whip.

The equipment comprises a felt poll pad fitted with a pulley
on either side and fastened over the headpiece of the bridle or
cavesson; a leather attachment, which separates into two arms
and is adjustable at the breast, is fastened between the forelegs
to a roller or surcingle in the same way as a martingale. The two
arms terminate in cords fitted with snap hooks. The cords slot
through the pulleys on either side of the poll pad and then pass
downwards to be clipped to the bit. (If it is intended to lunge
the horse in the device rather than to work it loose, a bit,
preferably one with a thick, soft mouthpiece, like a mullen-
mouth rubber snaffle, or one of flexible plastic, becomes an
essential and this is fitted to the usual light lunge cavesson.)

The effect of the Chambon is to cause a lowering of the head

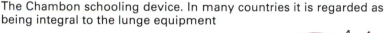

The Chambon schooling device. In many countries it is regarded as
being integral to the lunge equipment

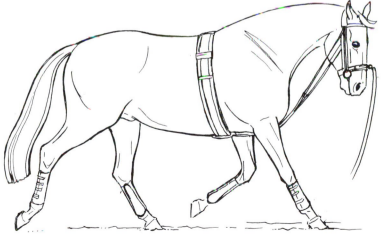

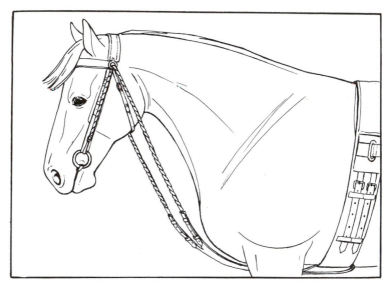

The effect of the Chambon is to lower the horse's head and neck

and neck. This, in turn, causes the shoulders to be raised, the back rounded and the hocks to be engaged more effectively under the body to establish a natural balance. In that process, the joints of hip, stifle and hock will be flexed strongly, and in time, of course, there will be a significantly rounded development of the upper muscles of the back and quarters.

Clearly, it can be used to correct horses who move with hollowed backs and have developed muscle on the underside of the neck rather than upon the crest (a ewe neck), but that is only one application. Used consistently with a young horse (or even in the re-schooling of an older one) it produces the correct rounded outline that is necessary for balanced, rhythmical movement, and it improves immeasurably the flexion of the joints. All this is achieved without force and with no risk of the mouth being damaged.

The Chambon is brought into play when the horse attempts to raise its head unduly and causes the cords to tighten.

However, it only limits the upward movement of the head, otherwise the horse is able to move its head and neck sideways, forwards and downwards without any restriction.

Should the horse attempt to lift its head above the acceptable level, the movement is countered by the bit moving *upwards* in the mouth – no *backward* pressure, restrictive of the stride and disturbing the balance, is possible. At the same time a gentle pressure is exerted on the poll at the nerve centre under the felt poll pad. (The weight method discussed earlier might have the disadvantage of numbing this nerve because of the constant pressure it exerts.) Once the horse has become used to working in the device, it quickly responds to these pressures by lowering its head, and the bit at once assumes its original position.

The Chambon is, indeed, a remarkably effective instrument, which can add a completely new dimension to the lunge work, but like everything else its success depends upon it being used carefully and intelligently. Particularly critical are the introductory work and the subsequent adjustment of the cords.

Initially, it is best to allow the horse to work loose within an enclosed space. The Chambon should be fitted so that the action only becomes apparent when the head is carried very high. It can then be tightened gradually, bit by bit and day by day, until it is sufficiently tight to cause the horse to carry its *poll in line with its withers and its nose on a level with its hip*. The horse will then start to move in the short, relaxed rhythmical trot that is the true gait of the Chambon and the one most rewarding in terms of balance and muscle development. In these early stages the schooling sessions should not exceed fifteen minutes. Any period longer than that will cause the muscles of the loin and thigh to ache, and that will be entirely counter-productive in both the physical and mental contexts.

Once the horse can be worked easily to either hand on the lunge rein, the training session can be increased by stages up to 30 minutes. During the last ten minutes the effect of the Chambon can be increased by tightening the equipment by a hole or two in order to make the horse really use its back when it is *sent forward* from the whip. This, of course, is the secret. To obtain the full advantage of the Chambon, the whip has to act in the same way as the rider's legs do when the horse is being ridden. It must push the horse forward into an increased contact with the hand via the lunge rein.

Cantering on the lunge must always be approached with great care.

This gait is far less productive than the trot, which encourages a much fuller use of the body. When using the Chambon, cantering should not be attempted until the horse has become confirmed in trot and that will take *not less* than two months and possibly even a week or two longer than that, depending on the adaptability of the horse and the skill of the trainer.

Because at the outset the horse will naturally carry its head higher in canter, the equipment must be loosened again, once more being tightened up gradually until the normal position has been reached. The 'normal' position will, of course, vary from one horse to another.

Very occasionally, one comes across a horse that, while lowering its nose well enough, evades the action by arching its neck. According to one of the greatest exponents of Chambon training, Yves Benoist-Gironière, the solution is to cross the cords across the face, fastening the off-side one to the near-side bit ring and vice versa.

(Benoist-Gironière wrote *The Conquest of the Horse*, where he quotes Colonel de Galard as his authority for the crossed rein method, claiming that it 'often yields considerable success with horses who try to evade the bit or who hold back'. He emphasises, however, the need to apply active legs when mounted at any time, and to push the horse forward energetically with the whip when schooling from the ground.)

When considering the Chambon, which, it has to be emphasised, is only used in lungeing and *never* under saddle, it is salutary to recall the words of another gifted trainer and teacher, Anthony Paalman, the author of *Training Showjumpers*. He wrote:

Correct lungeing with the Chambon improves *every* horse. Lungeing is a necessary, as well as an important part of the training of a showjumper. But, regrettably, it does more harm than good when executed incorrectly. *If the horse is just*

running around on the lunge, the lungeing is a waste of time.
(The last italics are mine.)

Less well known, less precise and probably less effective is the
so-called **continental martingale**, used extensively in the European circus. It differs from the Chambon in that downward
pressures are applied on the poll and nose, rather than to the
bit, but it has the same objective.

6: Jumping on the Lunge

This is a valuable exercise for teaching the horse how to gauge its fences for itself (with appropriate help from the trainer in the matter of the approach, and the trainer's intelligent use of a distance or placing pole, which will automatically put the horse in the right stride). The horse learns how to use itself over a small fence and gains confidence in its ability as a result. It is even possible at a later stage to teach it to jump simple combinations and, of course, varying types of fences, as long as the obstacles are kept low and the horse is not over-faced at so early a stage in its career. Moreover, it learns to jump without the inhibiting weight of the rider and without the rider risking confusion as a result of trying to influence the leap.

It is a wise precaution to rest a pole on the top of the upright, with its other end on the ground towards the take-off side of the fence. The pole should extend at least 45 cm (18 in) beyond the top of the upright. The purpose of this pole is to prevent the lunge rein becoming caught up on the upright, an occurrence that would do no good to the horse's confidence and would effectively destroy its trust in the trainer. The pole also acts as a wing to discourage any idea of running out.

Poles can, indeed, be regarded as training aids in themselves – 'Give me a pole and I'll make you a horse' was a favourite saying of one distinguished French trainer.

Good heavy poles, laid 1·3–1·5 m (4½–5 ft) apart to form a trotting grid, constitute an excellent balancing and strengthening exercise and can be used as an introduction to jumping. The grid can also be regarded as a means of regulating the length of stride, the latter being made to lengthen or shorten according to the distance between the poles. It is therefore a way of developing the horse's ability to adjust its stride according to the circumstances presented – a very necessary accomplishment in the competition horse. Raising the poles from the ground, or substituting **cavalletti** at progressive heights, compels the horse to move with greater activity, raising its legs higher and increasing the flexion of the joints. (The British Horse Society does not 'recommend' the use of cavalletti because it is possible to cause an accident if they are piled one on top of another to form a fence – as would be the case with any fence that is not constructed properly or with safety in mind. However, although that point is arguable, used in the accepted ground exercises the cavalletti remains one of the most versatile and valuable training aids and it would be nonsensical to regard its use in any other light.)

For the first jump on the lunge, the penultimate pole or cavalletto is moved up to join the last pole to make a little spread fence that will be jumped easily out of trot.

To prevent the horse rushing its fences and to provide some assistance in judging the take-off point, **distance** or **placing poles** are employed in the jumping training under saddle. A pole placed 5·4 m (18 ft) in front of a fence will allow one non-jumping stride in canter between it and the obstacle. A distance of 10 m (33 ft) allows two strides and 13·7 m (45 ft) three.

Duration of Work on the Lunge

The duration of work on the lunge has to be increased gradually. At the outset, fifteen minutes is quite enough for a young horse who has yet to learn co-ordination in its movements and whose muscles etc. are undeveloped.

Thirty minutes on the lunge is hard going for a mature horse. Following a session of that length it would be possible to spend a few minutes on grid work or jumping, but only in the later stages of the elementary training.

The lunge is a valuable training aid in the right hands and a dangerous one otherwise. It is quite possible to ruin a young horse's action forever, probably as well as its temper, by injudicious and inexpert lungeing. The fault usually lies in working for periods that are too long, and insistence on tight (and potentially very damaging) circles. Muscles then run the risk of being over-strained, the horse is forced into making resistances in order to mitigate the discomfort it experiences, and the stride becomes shortened, probably forever.

7: *Système de Gogue*

The Chambon is a relatively sophisticated piece of equipment when compared with basic lungeing tackle. Its use, however, whether schooling young horses or dealing with older ones that have been spoilt by inexpert handling, is confined *solely* to the lunge exercises. It can be argued, with justification, that a lungeing exercise carried out in the Chambon will produce a more correct muscular development and a better working outline than is normally possible using conventional methods, but thereafter both those desirable attributes must be maintained and extended by work under saddle. With riders that are both skilful and knowledgeable, no more than the occasional, if inevitable, hiccup in the training programme will occur, although occasionally older horses may attempt to revert to previous habits when the restraint imposed by the apparatus is removed. In these circumstances it will be necessary to return to the Chambon and its corrective influence. Indeed, many trainers who use the apparatus consistently will continue working on the lunge to provide a supportive grounding to the ridden work.

In a sense, the **de Gogue** can be regarded as an expansion and extension of the principles involved in the use of the Chambon, but it would be wrong to regard it as no more than an improved version of the latter. It adds yet another dimension because it can be used in an unbroken training progression both in the lunge *and* in the ridden work. The advantage of this consistent element throughout and even beyond the schooling period is obvious enough, and it is for this reason that the de Gogue deserves to be considered as a *system* rather than just an ingenious training aid.

In fact, although there are close resemblances between the

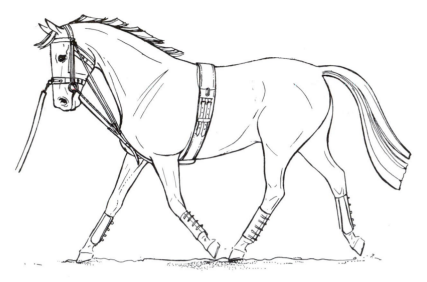

The de Gogue system (*above and opposite page*) is more versatile
than the Chambon and more wider-ranging in its effects

Chambon and the de Gogue, and a general agreement as to the
objectives to be achieved by their use, the de Gogue obtains its
results by the employment of somewhat different restraints,
which are possibly more precise and refined in their action.
Additionally, the greater versatility of the apparatus is capable
of producing far wider-ranging effects.

The device is the invention of the French horseman and
trainer René de Gogue and is based upon the recognition of
what de Gogue calls 'the three points of major resistance' in the
unschooled or badly schooled horse – the poll, mouth and base
of the neck.

To overcome the stiffness in these areas, the martingale (the
de Gogue can still be considered as a member of that family)
forms a triangle between the three points. Within the confines
of that triangle the horse learns to carry its head comfortably in
the required lower position. This is the 'independent' position
and is retained in the early ridden work. Initially, as with the
Chambon, it is advisable to work the horse loose, thereafter it

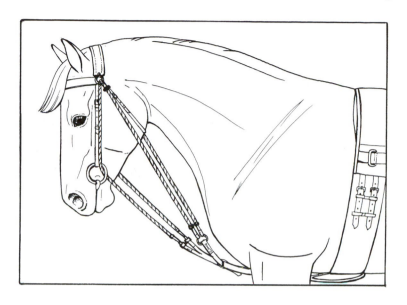

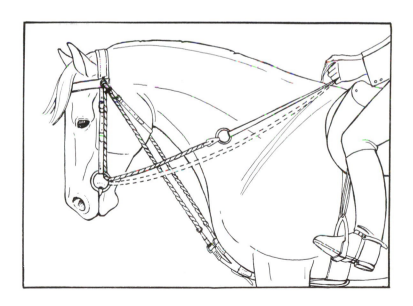

can be worked in the apparatus on the lunge line. As before, the effect is to raise the base of the neck, free the shoulder, produce greater engagement and flexion of the hock and encourage the muscled development of a rounded top-line.

It is at this point that the de Gogue goes a significant step further than the Chambon, being used more precisely to produce an advance in the head carriage as a result of greater flexion at the poll.

When the horse is moving freely and energetically in the required form, it is possible, by gradual stages, to adjust the apparatus in order to bring the nose inwards and increase the flexion at the poll. However, it must be done carefully and gradually and it is absolutely essential to insist on the horse moving forward with undiminished energy and freedom. The horse is unable to become overbent because of the stops fitted to the rein below the small pulley on the poll pad.

The next stage is to ride the horse with the martingale in the same independent position but with the addition of an ordinary rein to the bit ring, which in no way alters the established 'triangle of constraint'.

At the outset, it is advisable to loosen the martingale adjustment until the horse has become accustomed to moving with the weight on its back and is responding easily to the rider's legs. Once that has been obtained, the 'triangle' can be tightened again.

Finally, the rein can be attached to the cords in the 'direct' position. The triangle is now completed by the rein going directly to the hand – a very considerable advance on the limited use of the Chambon. Opinions vary as to whether an additional rein should be attached to the bit ring so that the de Gogue is operated in the same manner as a draw rein. In my view (and that of the de Gogue's inventor) it should not be necessary if the rider is experienced and effective but for anyone less confident of their ability it is a sensible addition and may also act as a useful introduction to the use of the single direct rein.

In fact, the extra rein used in the manner suggested is only directly applicable when schooling on the flat, for the de Gogue can be used for jumping and cross-country too.

With a horse schooled in this system, the rider obtains maximum control with the minimum of effort, the horse responding smoothly to the indications of the hand and performing with all the athleticism of which it is capable – an athleticism greatly encouraged by the correct and supple development of the form and musculature. In brief, that is what the de Gogue is all about.

A number of European riders have used the de Gogue in competition, one of the first being M. Rouffe of the Swiss horse trials team of the 1950s to 1960s, who rode his horse in the martingale at a number of international events.

A note of warning should, however, be sounded. This martingale, as well as the other schooling items described, is *not* within the province of the novice rider and it should not be used even by riders at a somewhat higher level than that without the supervision of an experienced instructor.

8: The Balancing Rein

Inevitably there has to be a discussion about the balancing rein perfected by the late Major Peter Abbot-Davies. This is probably the most controversial of all the 'auxiliary aids' produced within the last half-century.

Peter Abbot-Davies's rein was introduced over a decade ago and was vigorously promoted in the equestrian press and through public demonstrations given all over the country. Its inventor, a brave and skilful horseman, frequently demonstrated his rein personally and he also rode horses trained in the method in top-class jumping competitions. (In fact, Peter Abbot-Davies died 'in the saddle', falling from his horse in the Stoneleigh collecting ring, following a coronary, as he was waiting his turn to jump.)

The 'establishment', which had condemned the use of draw reins and related items and was bound to support the purist view, reacted predictably and strongly against the new rein. In hindsight, it may be that there was an over-reaction. If that was so, it was probably fuelled by the aggressive marketing methods of Abbot-Davies and then by the whole-hearted (and honest) endorsement of the product given by the international event rider Sue Hatherley, who wrote the introduction to the balancing rein instruction manual.

None the less, the rein survived the onslaught of the critics and today, over twelve years later, it is marketed successfully from a riding centre in Northampton devoted to its use. On that account, as well as for the reason that some notable riders achieve good results with it, it deserves consideration, or at least study, by serious – and fair-minded – horsemen and women.

The principle involved is very nearly as old as man's association with the horse. Evidence of the use of a rein

The balancing rein perfected by Peter Abbot-Davies. It is used today by some notable riders and there is a riding centre at Northampton devoted to its use

attached from mouth to tail can be seen in the carved depiction of chariot horses on the façade of the Temple of Rameses III at Medinet Habu, which is dated as belonging to the twelfth century BC. 'Tail-reining', as a counter to one-sidedness, has been practised in most parts of the world ever since, while variations on the running rein theme have been about for almost as long.

Abbot-Davies combined the two principles, mitigating what can be the inhibiting action of the draw rein by the use of a 'shock-absorbing' system based on an ingeniously contrived pulley and spring arrangement.

The object of the balancing rein system is to build up the

muscles of the back and upper neck in a relatively short space of time or, of course, to correct a faulty muscle structure (which is the object of most, if not all, of the schooling reins). In the process, the back is rounded, the quarters actively engaged under the body and the head and neck lowered, the former being strongly flexed. As a result the balance is improved immeasurably and it is claimed that this improved posture can be maintained thereafter when the horse is ridden in a simple snaffle. The pulleys counteract any tendency towards being one-sided and the spring action contributes to the softness of the hands.

It is further claimed that the system 'has a calming influence on even the most wayward of characters, never fails to position the horse correctly and it prevents all resistance'. 'I have ridden many horses in Peter Abbot-Davies's rein', wrote Sue Hatherley in 1977, '... and not one of these horses has objected to the fitting or using of the rope.'

The balancing rein can be used in three positions according to its adjustment on the rein

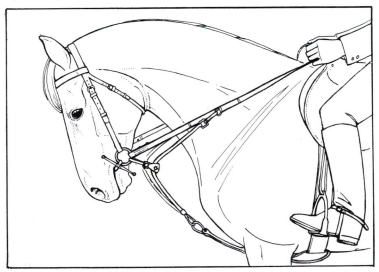

The rein can be used in three positions:

1 Attached from the mouth to the girth;
2 From mouth to tail with a rope that is passed through a soft sheepskin sleeve;
3 From the mouth to behind the ears by means of a rubber connection.

The last position can be used for mounted schooling but is more usually associated with lungeing. The effect is to produce an exaggerated lowering of the head and neck, which works the muscles of the neck and of the back and contributes to their development. Clearly, it must also produce an accompanying engagement of the hindlegs. This position can be used for the lunge exercises in conjunction with the second, mouth to tail, position.

The second position is, indeed, critical to the system and is employed at the outset to accustom the horse to the pressures of the rein and to produce the initial rounded outline. It has to be used sympathetically and sparingly. Two short initial lessons in Position 2 are sufficient to correct the position of the back and quarters, and thereafter it is advised that the rein need not be used in this position for more than one short period each month.

The everyday use of the rein is made in Position 1, when the attachment is from mouth to girth by means of a rubber rod. In this position the horse can be exercised, worked on the flat and jumped over fences up to 1 m (3½ ft) in height.

The advantages of what amounts to bringing together both extremities (the draw rein, remember, acts only on the front end) are obvious. It accomplishes a rounding of the *whole* frame and does so in a manner that is inescapable, but because of the rein's shock-absorbing, spring-loaded character, it is claimed not to create resentment, resistance or pain. Once the muscles are built up to comply with the imposed form, there can be no question of the effect not being maintained – the muscles hold the horse in the rounded outline and the movement, coming through from the engaged hindlegs, is bound to be improved and become freer. All this can be achieved in a short space of time – 'this patent rein will act as an accelerator, doing in one week what would normally take months of work'.

Are there any disadvantages in a system that obviously works and obtains results, at least for some.

In theory perhaps not, in practice there are dangers, principal among them being those involved with the rein's use in less than expert and very inexperienced hands that are accompanied by very effective legs. However, it can be argued that the same applies to any other training aid, even to the heavy-handed rider using a snaffle.

The rein compels the horse to work hitherto little used muscles throughout the body and to work them hard. As a result, even with the most experienced handler, the horse will be a bit stiff and perhaps a little sore in the initial stages of training. If the work is overdone, the horse may become *very* sore, which is unacceptable and will probably lead to deep resentment. Horses of other than good conformation could suffer pain and damage as a result of being made to work in the rounded form, for the rein cannot correct a natural malformation, nor, indeed, is any claim made on that score.

Much of the rein's value lies in it being fitted very precisely. The instructions given are clear enough but it would be possible for a novice to adjust the rein incorrectly.

The initial position of mouth to tail demands riding ability of a high order or the presence of a skilled trainer to supervise from the ground – anything less could be disastrous. In any case, anyone contemplating the use of the rein would probably be well advised to take a short course of instruction before embarking on a system demanding such a high degree of understanding and know-how.

9: Long Reins

In the training progression of a young horse, the lunge exercises form the lead-in to work on the long reins. Not all trainers, by any means, long-rein their pupils. Some hold that it is unnecessary and that the same results will be obtained from the saddle, while others do not long-rein for the very good reason that they have never mastered the art. Those that are adept with reins, however, can achieve excellent results in terms of obedience to the rein aid, improvement of balance and the refinement of the paces *before* the horse is asked to carry weight on its back. A horse that has been systematically conditioned and developed on the lunge and has then been taken on further in the long reins is well prepared for the work under saddle. Because it is physically strong, supple, balanced and obedient it will have little difficulty in working with a rider on its back and, very important, it is less likely to develop resistances in the early ridden stages in opposition to the rider's weight.

There are four methods of long-reining, of which the so-called **'English' method** is probably the least sophisticated but, equally, possibly the most practical for the purposes of the majority of trainers. Properly executed, it is indeed entirely effective. It is the only method of the four that requires the outside rein to pass round the quarters and to be used from that position to influence the movement. However, when a roller is employed and the reins pass through the rings, a skilful operator can practise a whole range of movements. Not only can the horse be driven on a circle to either hand at walk, trot and canter, but it can also be driven directly ahead with the trainer behind it, encouraging it to advance forward and come into contact with the bit. Furthermore, it is not very difficult to teach the beginnings of lateral work.

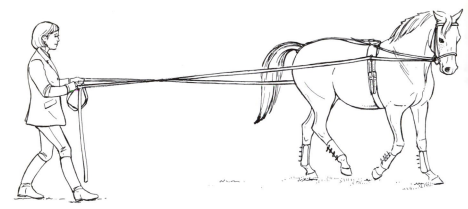

The English method of long-reining with the outside rein passing behind the quarters. It is the most practical method for the majority of trainers.

The French use this arrangement to drive the horse 'on the bit'

This method is less satisfactory when the horse is worked in a saddle with the reins passing through the stirrup irons. The work is then less precise, less finesse is possible in the handling of the reins and the whole thing smacks rather more of the rough and ready.

Long reins can be the same length and width as lunge reins, although many trainers prefer a lighter rein, like a plough line, so as to reduce the weight on the mouth. Swivel attachments are not necessary.

The specialist methods of long-reining apply to the advanced horse.

They are the **French method**, the **Danish manner** and what may be termed the **classical method**, exemplified in the gala performances of the Spanish Riding School.

The **French method** is based on the use of a harness driving collar.

The reins pass from the bit through the ring terrets on the collar and then downwards through rings placed midway on a breaking roller and from there into the hands of the trainer, who positions himself directly behind the horse.

By passing the rein through the roller rings, it comes to the hand at a convenient level, but, of course, the action is strengthened. The object is to assist the advanced horse in obtaining the high and near-vertical head carriage termed *ramener*, which is caused by 'the body advancing to the head', a matter made possible by the trainer pushing the horse into his or her hand.

The **Danish manner** has the reins running from the mouth, through the terrets of a harness driving pad and thence to the trainer's hand, the horse being worked on circles or directly to his front.

Experts, like the late Einar Schmit-Jensen and his pupil Miss Sylvia Stanier, can produce the full range of Grand Prix movements, including *piaffe* and *passage*, without the horse ever having had a rider on its back. Alas, this is outside the capability of all but the most skilful of trainers, and is not applicable to the majority of young horses.

If anything, the **classical method** is even further removed from the run-of-the-mill horseman. Of all, it is the most simple

The 'classical' long-rein method demonstrated by the Andalucian School. The horse, in this instance, is driven from a curb bit

method, the rein coming straight from the mouth into the hands of the trainer who works the horse from immediately behind and hard up against the animal's rear. Its purpose is to display, in hand, the paces and movements of the trained horse at the highest level.

10: The Controversial Draw Reins

The everyday martingales, both standing and running, have been discussed at length in the second book of this series, *Bitting*. In that they seek to position the head by imposing restraint on either nose or mouth, they have something in common with the more coercive and controversial draw or running rein. Indeed, a running martingale adjusted tightly enough to cause an angle in the rein between the mouth and hand, already has something of the nature of a draw rein, i.e. a rein to draw inwards. Used in conjunction with a second rein that is fitted above the one subject to the martingale action, on a large ring snaffle, the arrangement can be operated in much the same fashion as that advocated for the draw rein proper.

The Market Harborough

A closer relation to the latter but belonging to the same family group is the **Market Harborough**.

The draw rein is often referred to as 'the razor in the monkey's hand', and perhaps in that sense the Market Harborough can be regarded as 'the blunted razor'.

In Britain the Market Harborough rein used to be known as the 'German rein' because of its adoption by German show-jumping riders in the 1960s. At that time, with some justification, the Germans were calling it the English rein! There remains some confusion as to whether it is, indeed, a rein or a martingale. In fact, it has some of the properties of both and is either more or less martingale, or more or less schooling rein, depending upon how it is viewed and used by the rider.

Nor is the rein's origin very clear. It enjoyed a certain

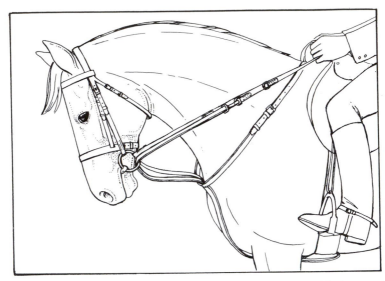

'The blunted razor' of the draw rein family, the Market Harborough

popularity in the 1950s when it was made in the West Country by a saddler named Vickery, but I believe it goes back to a time much before that. Something very similar was used in the schooling of polo ponies in India before the Second World War. More significantly, the late Count Robert Orssich, one of the greatest producers of hacks of all time, remembered that in his youth a schooling rein of this type was a common enough piece of equipment in both the civilian and military establishments of Hungary, formerly a part of the vast Austro-Hungarian Empire where classical equitation was well understood and practised.

It is probable that Count Orssich was remembering the running rein (*Schlief-Zügel*) introduced by Louis Seeger but which may, in fact, have been the invention of his mentor, Max von Weyrother. Seeger died in 1865 when the rein was in general enough use in the military schools of Europe. It was described in detail by Francis Dwyer in *Seats and Saddles, Bits and Bitting* etc., published in its revised form in 1869, and is referred to earlier in this book. In its original form, Seeger's rein

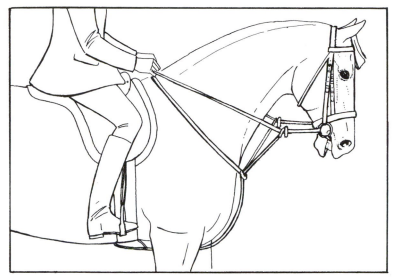

A straightforward running martingale if adjusted tightly has some of the properties of a running rein

was an instrument of considerably more strength when compared with the Market Harborough.

The construction of the Market Harborough varies a little from one manufacturer to another but in basic terms the equipment comprises the usual martingale body with the two branching straps, beginning at the chest, being longer and thinner than those employed in the ordinary running martingale. The two straps, sometimes made of either rawhide or rounded leather, are passed through the bit rings and are then fastened to the otherwise normal direct rein by small snap hooks connected to one or other of four metal dees fitted on the direct rein. Some patterns may use an adjustable buckle on the rein but this is not as neat as the snap hook and metal dee arrangement. Both methods, however, allow for a considerable degree of adjustment, which enables more or less restriction to be placed on the upward movement of the head. Additionally, of course, the adjustment can be used to encourage increased flexion at the poll.

Employed as a martingale, and the name Market Harborough

does suggest that it might have been regarded as a useful restraint for an over-exuberant performer in the hunting field, the action, though possibly more direct, is no more complicated than that of a running martingale. Should the horse either throw or carry its head unacceptably high and, in consequence, come out of the hand's control, the leather strips passing through the bit rings tighten, causing the bit to exert a downward pressure across the lower jaw. The severity of the device is, of course, limited by the adjustment. There is no doubt that the rein acts as a very effective means of restraint in this context, but if adjusted *too tightly* and used by a pair of less than competent hands, it could result in the desirable extension of head and neck over a fence being restricted and might encourage the horse to jump with a hollowed back. Like every other piece of equipment used on the horse, it is no substitute for good riding.

The other function of the Market Harborough, as a schooling rein, is more sophisticated. Regarded in this light it is really a watered-down version of the running rein and because its effect can be limited by adjustment it has a less damaging potential in the hands of the less than expert rider. In certain circumstances it could be used for a short time by a pupil under supervision, to place the horse into a more effective working frame.

The way in which the rein is best employed is for it to be adjusted loosely at the outset and then gradually, and carefully, tightened. As long as the horse flexes at the poll, drops its nose and relaxes its lower jaw, it will be ridden on the direct rein. Only when it comes out of that position and above the bit does the horse experience the correcting pressure across the jaw exerted by the lowering reins passing through the bit rings. With a normally sympathetic rider, the horse realises very quickly that submission brings immediate comfort to the mouth. The advantage of this rein is that it is so much easier for the rider to obtain a result within the limits imposed by the adjustment and so much more difficult for it to be misused (hence the description 'blunted razor').

As with any device or bitting arrangement that has a direct effect on the position of the head and the relationship of the hand to the mouth, this rein becomes non-productive, and usually counter-productive, unless applied in conjunction with

active and effective legs. It is absolutely essential that the horse
should 'advance into his mouth and hand' as a result of the
rider's legs pushing the horse forward from actively engaged
quarters. (The danger in any sort of rein acting on the head
position is in neglecting this basic equitational truth and seeking
to impose a carriage through the hand alone. When that
happens the horse shortens the neck and the stride, resists in the
back, comes on the forehand and will almost certainly not be
straight, as it will seek to evade by swinging its quarters outside
the track of the forefeet.)

The Draw or Running Rein

The draw or running rein (which, though closely related, to the
Market Harborough is by no means the same thing) is for the
most part condemned by the equestrian governing bodies
although the German National Equestrian Federation is more
tolerant, allowing that certain circumstances 'may justify the
temporary use of running reins (mainly as a time saving effort)'
but only with horses of an 'extremely difficult conformation'.

If only by implication, toleration is also extended to the
temporary use of the rein in teaching the *Schaukel*, the seesaw
movement of backward and forward steps made without the
intervention of a halt.

As draw reins are used on a temporary basis by skilled
professional horsemen, despite the protestations of official
bodies, it is not unreasonable to assume that some advantage is
derived from their use by horsemen of that standing. Whether
such results are obtainable by the less experienced is very
improbable.

Before examining the expert use of the rein, it seems
necessary,
1 To define what is meant by the draw and running rein and to
   differentiate between the two;
2 To consider their purpose and examine the disadvantages of
   their use by the less than expert rider.

A **draw rein** originates at the girth, passes through the
forelegs and thence through the bit rings to the hand.

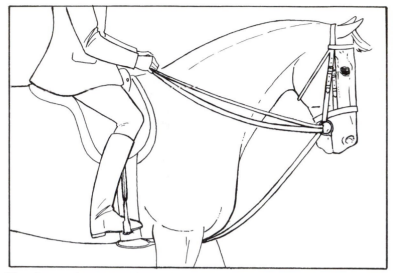

The draw rein passes from the girth via the bit rings to the rider's hand. In consequence its action differs slightly from that of the running rein

Newcastle's running rein persists in virtually the same form as when it was first used over 300 years ago

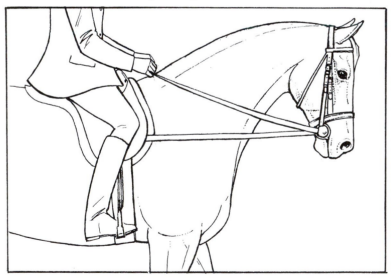

A **running rein**, the invention of the English master William Cavendish, Duke of Newcastle (1592–1676), and in common use throughout the most glorious period of 'classical' equitation, is fastened under the saddle flaps before returning via the bit rings to the rider's hands. In both instances, the rein is passed from the inside to the outside of the bit ring, a method that reduces, if only to a degree, the inward squeezing action that is more noticeable when the rein is fitted in the opposite fashion.

There is a difference in the action of the two. The draw rein, 'drawing' the head downwards as well as causing the nose to be retracted, is more direct in its action. The running rein will also cause the nose to be brought inwards, but places less emphasis on the lowering of the head.

The purpose of the reins is to assist in shortening and rounding the outline. A lowered head position is obtained by the horse coming increasingly onto the bit and it follows that any evasion contrary to that objective is countered. The ideal is for the rein to achieve its ends by *suggestion*. Obviously, however, it can be used to obtain a position by *force*, which must lead us to a consideration of the rein's disadvantages.

The inexpert rider, with less than very effective legs, may forget that the rein is no more than a very momentary means to an end. He comes to rely on it, using his legs to even less effect, and is deceived into thinking that he is creating a shortened outline. What is happening is that the horse shortens in front but, because of the lack of leg, it then fails to shorten behind by engaging its hocks under its body. Its balance is tipped down onto the forehand and if the rider persists with the rein the horse suffers aching neck muscles, which it seeks to relieve by tucking its head in still further to get behind the bit and which, in the end, make it sour and resentful.

In certain circumstances there is a place for the draw rein, as the German Federation acknowledges. Horses that evade by hollowing the back and lifting the head as a result of bad schooling and/or conformational defects can be corrected quite swiftly by its proper use.

Nearly every young horse, when it reaches that point in its training where it is asked to work within a frame created by its rider's legs and hands, will seek to avoid the restraint. It will swing its quarters in and out, throw up its head, duck its nose, twist at the poll or try one or more of another dozen similar ploys.

The purist answer, and the correct one, is to ask a very little at a time. The legs push the horse into the lightly squeezing fingers. It relaxes the jaw, drops the head and works within the frame for a few strides and is then released. Little by little the number of strides within the frame is increased and so it goes on. But this takes time, sometimes time out of all proportion to that which is available and once in a while there is the horse that persists in its resistance and seems to become ever more determined to evade the requests of its rider.

Even then, the rein should not be used as a short cut and certainly not to make up for failings in the basic training – that only confirms the defects forever. None the less, there is no denying the usefulness of the rein in helping the horse to understand what is wanted of it and to encourage it to submit willingly to its rider's legs and hands.

The draw rein, passing between the forelegs, is *always* used in conjunction with a direct rein fastened to the bit ring. It is held about 5 cm (2 in) shorter than the direct rein and comes into play against the bars of the lower jaw when the rider pushes the horse into the bridle. In response, the horse drops its nose and comes back onto the direct rein. The draw rein then remains inactive until the horse raises its head to come above the direct rein, when it once more exerts its downward pressure on the mouth. The horse soon learns that when it drops its head and accepts the direct rein, it is rewarded by the pressure of the draw rein being eased.

Constant use of the draw rein will produce nothing other than constant resistance.

Used in the way suggested, it is held that the horse quickly learns to lower its head, relax its jaw and flex its poll the moment it feels the rider's legs pushing forward to the hand.

Seeger's rein

Seeger's rein (used with a direct rein from the bit) employed a

The *Schlief-Zügel* rein
(*right*) was introduced by
Louis Seeger, the pupil of
Max von Weyrother. It was
in common use in the
nineteenth-century cavalry
schools of Europe. The draw
rein (*below*) in position.
Most trainers advise the use
of a drop-noseband with a
draw rein to prevent the
pressure being evaded by
the horse opening its mouth

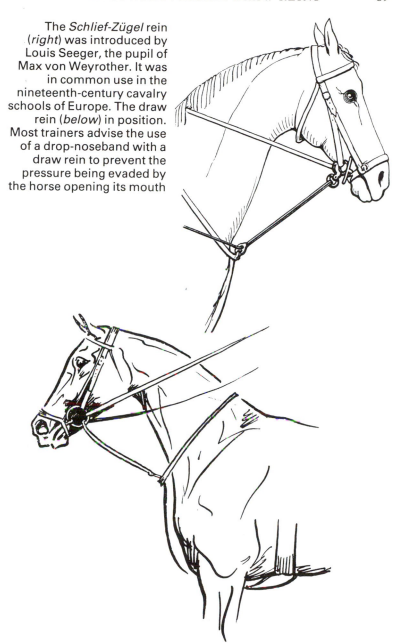

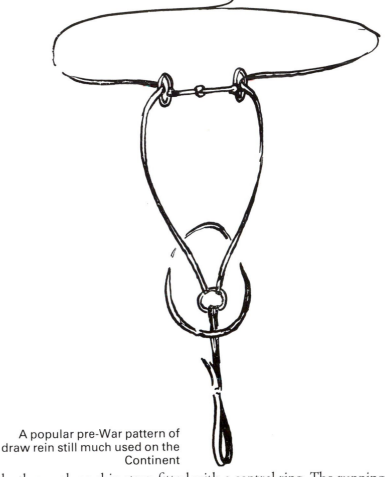

A popular pre-War pattern of
draw rein still much used on the
Continent

leather curb or chin strap fitted with a central ring. The running
rein was, in fact, operated by the *right* hand only. It was
fastened to a dee on the near-side of the saddle, then through a
martingale ring at the chest (from rear to front). From there it
went through the ring on the curb strap from left to right, back
again through the martingale ring at the chest (from front to
rear) and then to the rider's right hand. To quote Dwyer:

It is evident that a pull on this running rein will act directly on
the mouthpiece, drawing it back and somewhat downwards

towards the horse's breastbone; the great value of the whole arrangement being, that by taking the running-rein and right snaffle rein into the right hand, and the other snaffle rein into the left, we can place the horse's head in any position we desire and get a pull on the horse's mouth either horizontally upwards or downwards as may seem expedient.

He concludes: 'The advantage as compared with other running reins is that the position of the horse's head depends on the length of rein grasped and not on the force applied.' That was Mr Seeger's ingenious solution but he, of course, was far from being a 'monkey' and in his hands the rein was far from being a 'razor'.

11: The 'Artificial Aids' – Whip and Spur

The whip is certainly a training aid but it is also the horseman's wand of office. In an often ornamented form it was for long regarded as part of the warrior's regalia and no self-respecting steppe horseman would ever have thought of riding a horse without one.

Similarly, no driver of a wheeled carriage, from antiquity to the present day, would regard his turnout as being complete without a whip. Indeed, in the driving context, a whip takes the place of the legs of the mounted horseman and is an indispensable piece of equipment. The driver of any sort of carriage is often called a 'whip'.

The traditional material for a driving whip in Western countries is holly, as it has been for centuries, but in modern riding-whip manufacture materials like nylon and fibre-glass are used almost exclusively and today's whips are probably better than those of the past; they are certainly lighter and better balanced.

In pre-plastic days, steel-core whips were common in the middle price range, but if used to correct a horse, or to encourage it in a race, for instance, they left ugly marks and weals on the body. The best of the old materials was whalebone and a good whalebone whip from a top-class maker was a much prized possession. However, whalebone largely disappeared from the market when the killing of the Greenland whale, the principal source of supply, was prohibited by international law in 1946, and none of us will quarrel with that. Cane of all types is used to make hacking and show sticks, and one old and well-tried favourite is still available – the racing or jumping whip made from twisted nettle vine.

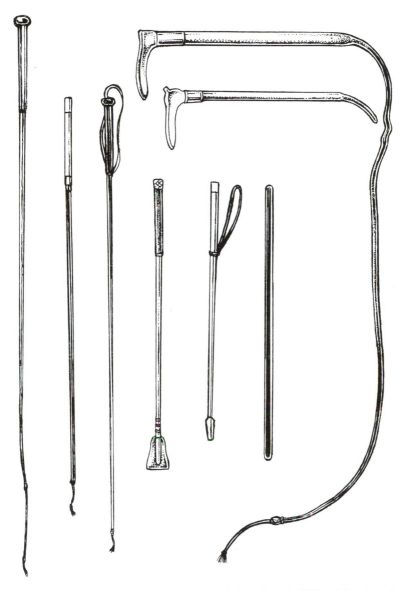

A whip for all reasons. The child's 'twig', or 'toothpick', with a hand-loop (*second from right in the centre row*) is 'a ridiculous and potentially dangerous item'

The riders of the Spanish School carry the long birch whip of classical equitation. It is used, certainly, as a practical aid but it also serves as a symbol of the rider's humility, which is a pleasing thought.

Lunge Whips

The purpose of the lunge whip is to act as an extension of the hand, pushing the horse from behind into contact with the cavesson rein. It is usually swept along the ground behind the horse, although it may on occasions be applied, tactfully, below the hock as a mild stimulant. Should the horse 'fall in' towards the centre of the circle, the whip, pointed at the shoulders, corrects the fault. It is never used, or *should never* be used, to hit the horse, but it may be cracked to tell the sluggard to mend its ways.

To meet those requirements and to fulfil its function as a training aid used from the ground, it needs to be sufficiently long and to be fitted with a thong that is a good bit longer than the stock.

Finally, the thong has to culminate in a lash made of whipcord or something similar. Without a lash it is impossible to crack a whip.

Hunt Whip

Whether a hunting whip (never a *crop*, which is either part of a chicken or the produce harvested from a field) is a 'training aid' or even an 'artificial aid' is doubtful, except when it is used *in extremis* to persuade a horse to take on some hairy obstacle. It is, however, cracked by hunt-servants when checking or rating hounds and is therefore equipped with a heavy thong and a strong whipcord lash.

The addition of a lash is entirely practical on both a lunge and a hunting whip but why it should have persisted, even in a shortened form, on the end of cutting, dressage and polo whips, where it serves no useful purpose at all, is something of a mystery and the only explanation obtainable from whip-makers is the time-worn and very unsatisfactory: 'It has always been made like that.'

Dressage and Schooling Whips

A dressage whip should be long enough to be used from the saddle without taking the hand from the rein, or to be used as a schooling whip on the ground when leading in hand, teaching the horse collection from the cavesson, etc.

From the saddle, it reinforces the leg by being tapped on the flank, or it may be used in a tap down the shoulder to encourage greater effort or to counter resistances in that part. Obviously, too, like all whips, it may be used, judiciously, for the purpose of correction.

Once more, however, it needs to be long enough, otherwise the horse may be jabbed in the mouth when the whip is applied behind the rider's leg. Furthermore, it needs to be fairly rigid, more rigid, in fact, than flexible. If it is too whippy it is likely to beat a tattoo on the animal's side rather than delivering a single, decisive tap.

Sometimes, one will see a rider with an extra long whip, long enough for him or her to be able to touch and activate the hock. In fact, this rider, all unconsciously, is using a type of driving whip, in effect a 'buggy' whip, but if it serves the purpose, despite being more whippy on account of the increased length, there can be no argument against its use.

Whips of this sort are always carried in the inside hand when riding in an arena or school, i.e. left hand on the circle left and vice versa. This is because the emphasis is on the inside, driving leg; we are, in fact, riding from the inside leg into the outside hand. If the whip is to support the leg, it has, therefore, to be carried in the inside hand.

Another practical reason for carrying the whip in this way when riding in a school is to prevent it from hitting the wall, something it would surely do if carried in the outside hand.

Polo whips, covered in plaited kangaroo hide, with a stout button on the top and a wrist loop – both to ensure that it does not slip from the hand – are purely pragmatic in their nature.

They are carried to make the pony lay its legs to the ground as fast as it can.

Jumping and Racing Whips

These whips are much shorter than schooling whips, the permitted length of a jumping whip being 75 cm (29½ in). Usually, the whip terminates in a broad flap that will make a satisfactory slapping noise when applied but will not cut. This whip is used to deliver a crack down the shoulder or, when greater effort is required, a swipe behind the saddle which, of course, entails the rider removing his or her hand from the rein.

Such whips are almost exactly like those carried by the fierce,

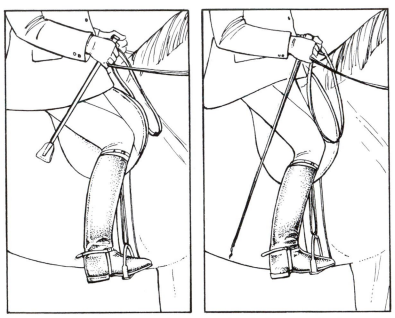

The jumping whip and the dressage whip held correctly. It can be seen how the latter can be used to reinforce the leg aid

steppe horsemen, who were the terror of the settled communities of their day, and who often used their whips in very much the same way.

A **'cutting' whip**, a term not now much used, is longer, although not as long as a dressage whip. Usually it is an altogether more elegant piece of equipment, although it is still practical enough.

For the side-saddle rider such a whip can act as a substitute for the inactive right leg.

A useful **hacking whip** is a stout type of cutting whip fitted with a horn handle, like a hunting whip, in order to facilitate the opening and closing of gates. A practical accessory to the handle is a small brass screw fitted into the base end. It gives greater purchase when pushing a gate and prevents the handle from slipping.

Otherwise, for hacking and showing, a **'cane'** is carried, which can be leather-covered or plain. A half-round, leather-covered cane, i.e. one that has been split so that one side is flat, is thought to lie more easily in the hand. More distinctive is the **'switch'** (stick) of holly, cherry or birch, carefully cut and nicely dressed and polished.

Children's Whips

In the trade these are called 'twigs'. My own description for these ridiculous and potentially dangerous items is 'toothpicks', although they would be equally as useless if asked to perform that function!

The objection to these riding 'twigs' is the hand-loop fixed at about the three-quarter mark so that the top of the whip projects by a good 15 cm (6 in) above the rider's hand. In the first place, the whip, as a whip, is then rendered useless because it is now too short to be used. Second, and more important, it could be dangerous when jumping or if, for some reason, the rider lost his or her balance or seat, even if only temporarily. In these circumstances it is possible for the end of the whip to stick upwards into the face or, worse still, into an eye.

So why are such whips manufactured? – 'We've always made

them like that!' My advice to parents would be to cut the wrist loops off.

Spurs

The purpose of the spur in practical terms is

1 To sharpen or refine the horse's response to the very lightest action of the leg;
2 To reinforce the leg's action;
3 To act as a correction when that is required – which *should be* infrequently;
4 For a purely cosmetic effect – a boot is always set off to better advantage when fitted with a spur.

Properly used by an educated horseman, spurs become no more than an extension of the leg. They are then a quite legitimate aid, and entirely humane, far more so than those vulgar, bruising kicks. (Indeed, the object is to make less and less use of the spur as the horse's schooling progresses.)

Whatever type of spur is worn, unless it be a dress spur, which snaps into a spur 'box' on the heel of a uniform boot, it is worn on the counter of the boot, i.e. where the boot's foot meets the leg.

The most common pattern is the **Prince of Wales**, which has a relatively short, drooped and blunt neck. The length of the neck is governed by the rules of showjumping, but more latitude is allowed outside that sport. In practice long-legged riders will need to wear long-necked spurs, if the spurs are to be effective, while riders of an opposite conformation need only a short necked spur.

The neck can, of course, be straight, which increases the potential severity, and some European spurs have squared necks, culminating in a point. In my view these are no more acceptable than the neck that is set on the inside of the heel.

Sharp points (i.e. inset with a rowelled wheel) will clearly be more severe and could be used to abuse the horse. Blunted rowels, despite their fearsome appearance, are probably not as severe as they seem as long as the leg is an educated one.

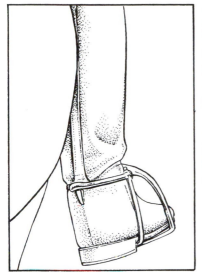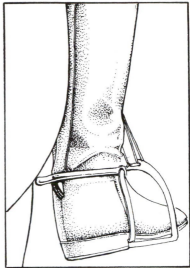

The usual Prince of Wales spur worn on the counter of the boot

The leg aid, whether applied with or without a spur, is made with a *forward* squeeze in a slight rolling manner that can be emphasised to the point where the foot moves a little outwards. The action causes the arm of the spur and, if the action is continued, the neck itself, to brush against the lay of the hair. The horse is sufficiently sensitive in this area for that to be quite enough to obtain the required response. When the leg is laid flat against the horse to control the shift of the quarters, only the metal arm of the spur comes in contact, unless the foot be turned a little outwards.

Surprisingly, the horse-peoples of Asia never employed the spur, relying entirely on their whips. Both Greeks and Romans, however, employed a short, prick spur worn on the heel. By the Middle Ages, long-necked, hugely rowelled spurs, were in favour and were necessary if the mounted knight of Western civilisation, who turned his horse by the leg, was first to reach his mount's flanks and second, to stimulate animals that became increasingly heavy and common.

It was, none the less, the spur that came to symbolise the ideal of knightly chivalry (*cheval* = horse, *chevalier* = horseman), and it was central to the ceremony of knighthood in an age when the knight was the embodiment of the Christian virtues. He 'won his spurs' after a night-long vigil spent in prayer, and even now the spur retains much of its symbolic status within ceremonial regalia. Its practical use should likewise be in keeping with the courtesy of chivalry.

12: Restraint – Management Aids

It is a fact that more accidents take place in stables, from kicks, bites, etc., than anywhere else. There is never a place for treatment that is rough and cruel but there are occasions when *principles* must take second place to the needs of *safety*.

Sometimes a horse has to be restrained for its own good and that of its handlers. It may, for instance, be necessary to exert a firm control over the horse's movements when first aid or veterinary attention is required, or in some instances when the horse is being clipped or shod. (Any form of restraint may be regarded as an admission of failure in the relationship between ourselves and our horses but so long as people impose domestication (which is an unnatural state) on the equine species, restraints are likely to be needed. When we cease to make use of the horse, we sign its death warrant. The choice is that simple.)

The Leg Strap

The simplest form of restraint, which is usually sufficient when clipping a normally tractable horse or handling it in some other way, is to lift a foreleg, holding the foot lightly in the *finger tips* so that the horse cannot put its weight on the hand and use it as a base from which to let fly with a hindleg.

Rather more salutary is the **leg strap**, which keeps the knee flexed by attaching the pastern or the cannon to the forearm. It can be made up specifically for this purpose, with loop and buckle, or a stirrup leather can be pressed into service. When using this measure it is prudent to fit kneecaps in case the horse should fall.

A strapped-up foreleg will usually frustrate evil intent

whether the horse is being clipped or shod. It is sometimes necessary, however, to control a hindleg. This can be done very easily by using a soft rope sideline (stiff, hard rope would gall the horse) that is knotted round the neck and fastened with a quick-release knot. The rope is then passed between the forelegs and round the hindleg (the one on the opposite side to the one that is being clipped). The end of the rope could be held directly by an assistant or it could be passed through the neck rope before going to his or her hand. Ideally, it is best to use a padded hobble on the pastern and to run the rope through a strong dee attached to this.

To prevent the horse striking with its forelegs or rearing, a half-sack of corn or feed nuts tied round the neck to hang just above the knees is an almost sure deterrent.

The Twitch

A twitch of one sort or another is still standard equipment in most yards and is a recognised and commonplace form of restraint.

It is applied to the nose, or rather the upper lip, and in its simplest form it is just a stout stick, about 30 cm (1 ft) in length, with a hole drilled through the end. A loop of twine or rope is passed through the hole and is put round the lip (avoiding the nostrils) until it is tight enough to be effective (a soft cotton rope is obviously milder in its action than a loop of baler twine, which could cut into the flesh). A handler either holds the stick or it can be pushed back through the side-piece of the headcollar. A 'humane' twitch is made from a pair of jointed wood or shaped metal handles that can be closed on the nose and fastened together at their extremities.

For many hundreds of years, possibly from the beginning of domestication, horsemen were well aware that the control of an animal as big and as strong as a horse was made easier if one could apply pressure on the upper lip. (Packs of wild dogs use the same principle when hunting large herbivores. One or two members of the pack latch onto the quarry's nose while the rest pull down the strangely subdued animal.)

Horse-people like the early Scythians, naturally versed in

animal lore, and then, a few thousand years later, the American Indian on the other side of the world, discovered that the relaxing, soporific effect produced by twisting the nose resulted in submission, and one cannot imagine that those fierce warriors bothered their heads as to the reason why.

Much later in time it was suggested that the discomfort experienced at the body's extremity distracted the animal from whatever was being done to it elsewhere.

Today, learned folk tell us differently, basing their research on their knowledge of acupuncture/acupressure points. When pressure is applied to the nose by the twitch, substances called endorphins and encephalins are released into the brain. Like the drugs to which these substances are related, such as heroin, morphine, etc., they have a dulling, relaxing effect, causing the horse to become virtually sedated. (Pinching a fold of skin on the side of the neck, which is also an acupuncture point, has a similar but less subduing effect. A pinch in this area is also a useful counter to the horse that persists in jogging and far more effective in that respect than action with the reins.)

Twitching is only effective for short periods. If the device is left on too long its effect is reduced; it needs, therefore, to be used sympathetically.

The 'experts' seem to suggest that the horse may actually enjoy the experience of being twitched – an hypothesis that I cannot accept. In my experience horses that have been twitched do not exactly show great delight at the prospect of the treatment being repeated, even though they will submit once the twitch is in place. Those that have been twitched on an ear – *an entirely unacceptable practice* – are even less ready to accept the restraint and may, indeed, become almost incurably headshy.

A very old method of sedating a horse without the use of a twitch was to give it slices cut from a twist or plug of tobacco. This was 'chewing baccy' and it was rough, very strong and usually impregnated with molasses. The nicotine it contained acted as a sedative that was quite as efficient as any administered via the vet's syringe.

'Professor' Galvayne, not surprisingly, had his own twitch, consisting of a slip knot at the end of a piece of rope. The noose was adjusted round the poll and under the upper lip. It is sometimes called the **Cherokee twitch** and, when tightened, it works, as one would expect, very well.

The Barnum

A more sophisticated twitch is the Barnum (named after Barnum and Bailey's Circus), also of American origin. It is described in some detail by Yves Benoist-Gironière in his book *The Conquest of the Horse*, and goes much further than a simple aid to management. Indeed, Benoist-Gironière elevates it to the status of a schooling aid. In essence, it is not much different to the 'bridle' used by the American horse-tamer Jesse Beary and the psychology on which it depends is the same.

The Barnum is effective as a twitch for use on a restive horse but its real purpose is in dealing with the recalcitrant and difficult subject and the assertion of mastery over him. Bothering not at all about acupuncture points, it acts irresistibly between the poll and the mouth, even though the mildest of soft, rubber snaffles is used.

The Barnum is more or less the same thing as the bridle used by the American horse-tamer Jesse Beary to subdue difficult subjects

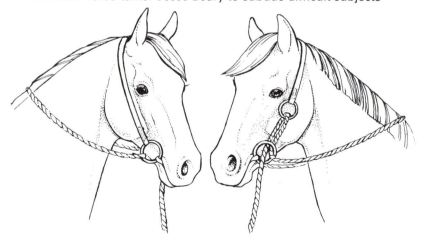

If the horse seeks to pull away, refuses to be led or is otherwise rebellious, the rein is pulled tight in a very strong, squeezing action. Inevitably, the horse turns to face the trainer. It may continue to fight for a few moments but in the end it submits and will quite suddenly drop its head and run into the trainer, who must quickly release the tight cord, making much of the horse as he does so.

Benoist-Gironière talks about the horse's 'obsession of the point of resistance' being broken and he quotes Gustave le Bon:

So long as there has been no struggle the horse cannot be totally convinced of his rider's authority. Only this struggle will convince him, and it is far better that it should take place at the start rather than later on. As soon as it is over, the animal will be disciplined and once he is disciplined in one respect, he will easily be so for all others. The battle is won, and from now on we need have recourse to nothing but kindness . . . a kindness which is quiet but never weak.

Sample, Galvayne, Rarey and Co. all met and broke resistance in difficult subjects, often termed 'vicious' or 'savage', by psychologically similar methods. They, however, relied upon hobbles and ropes to throw the horse down and keep it on the ground until it was released by its trainer, who had then asserted his authority in unmistakable fashion.

The Barrowcliff-Ellis System

Major H. Barrowcliff-Ellis trained Indian Army remounts and mules in the years immediately before the Second World War. In the eight years before the outbreak of hostilities, Barrowcliff-Ellis developed a system of schooling that he practised on over a thousand Australian walers (cavalry horses) and Argentine mules. These were animals that had been terrified and made dangerous by rough handling, herding and being thrown and branded, before being crammed into a ship's hold for an uncomfortable and bewildering sea journey. Barrowcliff-Ellis emphasised that his 'docility system' was neither applicable to,

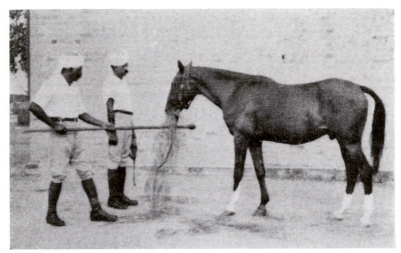

Using the blob stick as a safe introduction to handling. Galvayne termed this the 'third hand'

When the remount accepts the blob stick all over his forehand the foreleg rope is adjusted. The horse is then handled thoroughly over his head and forehand. With the foreleg rope in place the blob stick is passed between the hindlegs and round the quarters

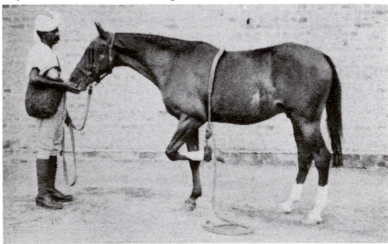

With the blanket apron and hindleg rope the horse can be handled
safely all over his body

nor necessary for, ordinary tractable animals, like those bred in
England or Ireland.

It was, he stressed, to be employed when the trainer was
faced

> ... with animals which kick, bite, refuse to be saddled or
> harnessed, jibbers, bolters, buck jumpers, refusing to stand
> still whilst being mounted, groomed or clipped, refusing to
> have the head, legs and ears handled or the dock sponged
> out, difficult to shoe or have wounds dressed, or which kick
> whilst out hunting ...

'It is', he averred, 'a positive cure for youngsters and more often
than not successful with old confirmed sinners'.

Barrowcliff-Ellis based his system on that of the German
trainer Lichtwark (to whom he gives the title 'Professor'), who
had settled in Australia in 1865. His system, however, was an
improvement on Lichtwark's somewhat rough methods, and his

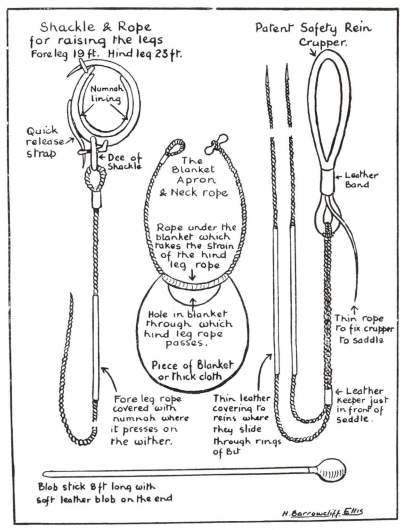

Shackle & Rope for raising the legs Foreleg 19 ft. Hind leg 23 ft.

Numnah lining

Quick release strap

← Dee of Shackle

Patent Safety Rein Crupper.

← Leather Band

The Blanket Apron & Neck rope

Rope under the blanket which takes the strain of the hind leg rope ↓

Hole in blanket through which hind leg rope passes.

Piece of Blanket or Thick cloth

Fore leg rope covered with numnah where it presses on the wither.

Thin leather covering to reins where they slide through rings of Bit

Thin rope to fix crupper to saddle

← Leather Keeper just in front of saddle.

Blob stick 8 ft long with soft leather blob on the end

H. Barrowcliff. Ellis

Barrowcliff-Ellis's tackle used in the training of remounts

tackle was all carefully padded to prevent galling. (Galvayne, Sample and Rarey may all have drawn from the same source. Certainly, Galvayne's 'third hand' is Barrowcliff-Ellis's 'blob' stick, which he inherited from Lichtwark.)

The blob stick comprised a pole that culminated at one end in a soft, stuffed pad, i.e. a blob, which simulated the touch of the human hand. Barrowcliff-Ellis's system first 'educated the head and legs' by strapping up a foreleg and getting the horse, with the help of rewarding titbits, to submit to the blob stick being passed all over the forehand. He then 'educated' the quarters in the same manner until the horse accepted the blob stick and the hand without demur and without the risk of the handler being injured.

His 'patent safety rein' was no more than a much improved

Galvayne's method of third-handling used to persuade the horse to submit to being handled – but in safety!

(*Above*) Barrowcliff-Ellis's Patent Safety Rein. He attributed it to the German trainer Lichtwark. Barrowcliff-Ellis claimed that it stopped bucking and other unruly behaviour and prevented bolting. In fact, it can be seen as a fore-runner of the modern balancing rein and makes similar use of the tail although over the top line; (*below*) The Patent Safety Rein being used to teach a horse to lead or trot out

version of Galvayne's harness and he used it to teach a horse to run out in hand and also as a cure for bucking. The illustrations illustrate the system quite clearly.

Hobbles and Picketing

Hobbles and pickets are not much used today but in the past cavalry horses on service were, through necessity, tethered side by side to a taut picket rope set at a height of 91–122 cm (3–4 ft) above the ground. (This method would still be relevant enough to a group of modern long-distance trekkers.) The length of the head-rope for cavalry horses was laid down in regulations as being the length from the back ring of the headcollar to the ground when the horse was standing up. The horses were further secured and prevented from kicking each other by a heel-rope fastened to one or both hindfeet. In the latter case, the V at the end of the rope was limited to a spread of 60 cm (2 ft), which was sufficient to allow the horse to lie down, get up and straddle in order to urinate. The heel-rope was attached to wooden or iron-shod pegs driven into the ground at an angle. The length of the heel-rope was laid down as being the taut, straight length from heel to heel-peg when the horse was standing up with his head directly over the picket line or head-rope.

Clearly, horses had to be taught to accept this sort of restraint, but in a group containing older horses that were well accustomed to being secured in this way little difficulty was experienced and, of course, the lines were always under the supervision of a picket guard.

When grazing, horses could be confined within reasonable limits by knee-haltering or by hobbles and both methods could appeal to present-day riders undertaking long-distance, non-competitive rides.

Hobbles are used to connect either both forelegs or a fore and a hind, the degree of movement being limited by the length of the rope between the hobbles.

Knee-haltering is accomplished by tying the head-rope from the backstay ring of the headcollar to the forearm just above the knee. The best knot to use is a clove hitch with a half hitch as a keeper to prevent the rope slipping. Once horses are used to this method, the rope can be secured fairly loosely either below the knee or round the pastern. The rope should in all instances be adjusted so that the horse can just reach the ground to graze, but it should not be longer than that.

Initially, horses should be taught to accept knee-haltering in a small, enclosed area that has a very soft surface, like the corner of an indoor school or an outdoor *manège*.

13: Correction of Vices

Crib-biting and Wind-sucking

Possibly the most serious of the so-called stable vices occurring in the domestic horse is that of crib-biting, a condition that frequently leads to the closely associated habit of wind-sucking. Both vices need to be declared if the horse is entered in a sale and no veterinary surgeon would issue a certificate of soundness for a horse suffering from either of them. Not surprisingly, both have a significant effect on the value of the horse.

A **crib-biter** will grasp any available object (the edge of a door or manger, for instance) with the incisor teeth and then grind them together whilst flexing the neck. Initially, there may be no ingestion of air but usually, in my experience, the crib-biter learns to gulp air into the stomach as an almost inevitable accompaniment to grasping the fixed object.

Wind-suckers swallow air in the same characteristic fashion but do not find it necessary to hold something in the teeth, although they may sometimes rest their chin on an object. Horses who are physically prevented from crib-biting may turn to wind-sucking.

Crib-biting can cause serious damage and excessive wear to the incisor teeth, which, as well as causing problems in the mastication of food, may result in dental disease. Excessive development of the muscle on the underside of the neck is brought about by its continual flexion and as, in advanced cases, the vice is practised almost continuously, the horse is rarely at rest. It then becomes difficult to maintain condition and a corresponding level of performance. In this respect, of course, the ingestion of air plays a significant part as it leads to abdominal discomfort and often to attacks of flatulent colic.

Crib-biting and wind-sucking are usually, and with some justification, regarded as 'highly contagious' habits and one crib-biter in a yard is almost certain to encourage others in the habit. (The advice usually given is to stable the crib-biter as nearly as possible in isolation, a practice that may, indeed, discourage would-be imitators, but does nothing for the crib-biter other than confirm it still further in the vice and possibly increase any tendency towards aggressive behaviour.)

Finally, the damage caused to stable fittings must be considered, and this, although not as extensive as the destruction wrought by wood- and fence-chewers, is still expensive. There is, of course, also the general and sustained inconvenience of owning a horse disposed to the vice.

Crib-biting and wind-sucking are almost entirely confined to the stabled horse. This vice does not occur in the wild and only very rarely when horses are turned out to grass. Crib-biters will, however, resume the habit when they are brought up and kept again in an enclosed environment.

The vice seems to be more prevalent in highly strung horses of a predominantly hot-blooded background, i.e. Thoroughbred and Arabian, but, conversely, that may be because such horses are more likely to be stabled and kept at relatively high levels of fitness.

Causes leading to crib-biting
The most common explanation given, other than contraction by mimicry, is that the vice is brought about by boredom arising out of the environment imposed by domestication. That may be true in part and in general but it takes no account of the specific environmental failings in either a social or physical sense. The problem is psychological and the solution, if and when it is found, is for the trained equine psychologist.

It helps if the horse is kept occupied as far as possible. A small-mesh haynet, for example, compels the horse to take time over eating the contents; a mangold in the manger will keep a horse similarly occupied, as will a salt lick. Stable toys are now available to serve the same purpose and it is not difficult to devise some of one's own. I am assured too, that, as with cows, 'music hath charms'.

The cure

Once crib-biting is established it is really incurable other than by surgery, and that is by no means always successful. All that can be done is to mitigate the condition as far as possible by careful stable management, which may well prove to be very time-consuming, or by implementing mechanical means to prevent the horse from indulging in the vice.

It is possible for the veterinary surgeon to remove portions of the neck muscle in order to make the horse incapable of flexing it. Sometimes this works and just as often it does not, nor is there any guarantee that there will not be a behavioural side-effect as a result. For instance, horses that are prevented from cribbing by mechanical means sometimes become more aggressive in their behaviour. (A noted authority, commenting on surgery, wrote, 'Horses crib-bite so their necks are cut – children suck their thumbs, so cut their thumbs off!').

The preventive devices available are quite numerous, and if we discount the fact that we are treating the symptom and not the disease and overlook the possibility of behavioural side-effects, they are for the most part effective, although not, of course, without their disadvantages.

This is Meyer's Pattern crib device which is humane and successful in the treatment of cribbers

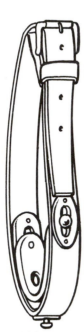

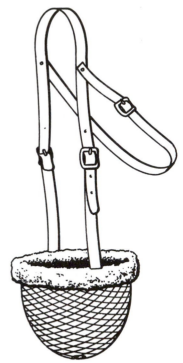

Cribbing strap (*left*) with inset metal spikes which prick the jowl when the horse's neck is arched in the act of crib-biting; (*right*) a stable muzzle. This type will prevent crib-biting (but not wind-sucking) and make life difficult for the confirmed bed-eater

The obvious answer in the case of the crib-biter is to remove all projections that the horse can grasp in its teeth. The door can be fitted with a wire mesh on the inside so that it cannot bite on the top of the lower door. That, of course, has the disadvantage of restricting the horse's view of the outside world and may increase its frustration and determination to persist in a different form of its chosen perversion – wind-sucking. Giving feed and water in thick-rimmed receptacles placed on the ground, from where it will be impossible for the horse to flex the neck muscle, is a sensible precaution. An electrified wire, of the type used in sheep fencing, is another solution, but the most common deterrents are the **muzzle** which has to be removed for eating and will not prevent wind-sucking, or the

leather neck strap, fitted with a gullet plate, which envelops the jowl tightly. Probably the most effective of all (if also the most barbaric) is the spiked variety in which a ring of metal spikes is fitted in the underside of the strap. When the neck is arched the prongs project and prick the jowl in a decisive and discouraging fashion.

Another device used on wind-suckers is the 'flute' bit and this is often successful. It consists of a hollow, perforated tube that remains fitted in the mouth while the horse is in the stable. The holes in the mouthpiece disperse the gulp of air and prevent it, at least in part, from being swallowed.

In the end, however, we come back to the inescapable fact that the 'vices' of cribbing and wind-sucking are psychological problems and the 'management aids' are no more than second-best solutions.

Weaving – Pawing – Box Walking

The development of stereotypes (aberrant behaviour repeated with monotonous regularity and fixed in all details) is an accompaniment of equine domestication. They arise from what may be termed environmental pressures and they are psychological in their nature.

Some stereotypes, like crib-biting and wind-sucking, are listed as vices and constitute an unsoundness. Obviously, they detract from the horse's value and if the horse is offered for sale the vendor is bound to declare the failing.

Weaving also comes into this category and, like the other two, has an adverse effect on the horse's physical condition.

A horse is said to weave when it continually shifts its weight from one foreleg to the other while waving its head incessantly from side to side. Because of this constant movement it is difficult to keep condition on the horse and it is possible that the strain caused to the muscles of the forelegs may have an effect upon the action. Furthermore, the habit is quickly picked up by other horses, which makes it necessary for the weaver to be kept isolated.

Weaving is a nervous complaint and the horse that indulges in the habit can hardly be considered as having a settled, well-balanced disposition. It is usually attributed to boredom (unless the habit has been contracted as a result of imitating a stable companion), and it occurs in a variety of animals, the chained circus elephant or even one kept in zoo conditions being a case in point.

It is doubtful whether weaving can ever be wholly eradicated once it is established but it can be contained to an acceptable degree by intelligent management.

'Mechanical' restraints comprise a V-shaped half-grille attached to the lower door of the stable, or, in its absence, a couple of heavy wood blocks suspended from the lintel and placed about 45 cm (18 in) apart in the doorway, the two ropes being connected by a thin cord placed 30–35 cm (12–14 in) above the blocks.

As, for the most part, weavers seem to prefer to put their heads over the stable door when indulging in their particular perversion, the grille, by containing the head and neck, prevents the characteristic sideways movement. For their part, the wood blocks will swing as they are struck by the swaying head and will, in turn, deliver what amounts to a fairly salutary 'clip round the ear'.

Both measures will discourage the weaving motion, but in essence all they are doing is preventing the physical manifestation of a state of mind, and that cannot be altered simply by a restrictive grille nor even by a clip round the ear.

Pawing
This is an irritating habit usually performed out of impatience, although it might be a sign of digestive discomfort.

Horses paw in anticipation of food and the solution is to keep them waiting for as short a time as possible.

Persistent stamping may be the result of itching heels caused by mud fever or, in summer, by the persistent harvest mite. A number of good proprietary remedies are available on the market or one can use the very effective udder salve made for cows.

Box-walking
Although not listed as a vice, this is a far more worrying habit,

which occurs most often in the hypernervous horse and is also very noticeable in caged animals. The horse circles the box continually, losing condition as a result and also wearing out its shoes. Everything that has been said about the weaver applies equally to the box-walker, but a change of environment and the provision of company that the horse can see and touch will often prove a successful remedy.

Old horsemasters and dealers sometimes tackled the problem by putting down an extra thick bed (up to twice the normal thickness) and then laying a number of car tyres on the top. I am assured it was entirely effective but I have never tried it and I suggest that unless you are very experienced you don't either.

(I have had one box-walker in my life. I cured him by giving him a bed up to his middle and conditioning him for hard work which, in his case, included a lot of jumping. While he was gainfully employed he never gave any trouble at all, but during a rest period he became the most irritable of creatures.)

Tying

The refusal to be tied up without resistance is not a failing included in the accepted group of 'stable vices'. None the less, it is an irritating behavioural problem, it can be expensive when leather headcollars are broken, and it can become a serious drawback in the day-to-day management of the horse. It may not be absolutely necessary to tie the horse up to be groomed or to clean out the stable but these tasks are simplified and carried out more quickly if the horse's head is secured so that its body can be moved from one side to another around that fixed point.

Usually, it is advisable to tie a horse when travelling and it may be necessary, at shows or on hunting days, to tie it to the outside of the box or trailer. (For the single-handed owner in those circumstances, reliability about being tied up is an essential requirement of any horse.)

Other than when at liberty in the paddock, the domestic horse is almost always under some manner of restraint. Even confinement in a loose box is a form of restraint. Properly handled from birth, however, horses develop an habitual acceptance of the restraints imposed upon them. None the less, we have to recognise that the act of tying a horse is in contravention of its natural defensive instincts. Despite its great strength, the herbivorous horse is a non-aggressive animal whose first line of defence is in swift and immediate flight. To put the animal in a position where it is denied a means of escape is bound to be fraught with potential dangers.

There are, I believe, horses who panic because of the claustrophobic effect induced by being tied up. Some will have run back against the tie rope because they have been startled and tried to escape an imagined danger. That is something that may occur with the steadiest horse at any time.

On the whole, properly brought-up horses will accept being tied up without problems arising. However, should a young horse evince anxiety or attempt to run back when it is first tied to a wall ring, there is, in my view, one almost infallible remedy.

Quite simply, you must *teach* it to stand quietly when tied. There is no guarantee that it will never attempt to run back under any circumstances – that would be too much to expect – but for ordinary purposes the horse will be as reliable as it is possible for an animal of its disposition to be.

The lesson should be taught in the stable, the trainer providing himself with a pocket of sliced carrots, an extra long tie rope and a soft grooming brush.

The rope is attached to the headcollar, passed through the wall ring and back to the trainer's left hand if he is operating on the horse's near side. The trainer then begins to groom the horse with the brush held in the right hand, commencing at the head in the usual way and working backwards while holding the rope a little shorter than would be usual.

At some point the young horse will try to take a step or two to the rear, while an older animal that is confirmed in the habit of pulling back against the rope, may attempt a more violent run-back. As soon as this happens, the trainer must allow the movement by giving the rope so that it slips through the ring and offers no resistance. The horse must then be quietly put back in its original position. It can be given a carrot and a pat and then grooming can be resumed. The same procedure is followed every time the horse moves backwards. In the course of one grooming session it may happen half-a-dozen times, but if the lesson is repeated every day for a week, the horse will come to understand what is required and will be quite happy to stand quietly when tied.

Sometimes, a horse that is known to run back will not do so under these circumstances, realising that it will gain no advantage from doing so. It is then permissible for the *experienced* trainer to provoke a minor resistance in order to get his or her message home. This is done by tightening the rope, ever so tactfully, as though to pull the horse forward. Invariably the horse reacts by pulling in the opposite direction and the corrective measures can then be taken so that the lesson is well and truly learnt.

While a horse is tied for grooming or for mucking out, it is always helpful if it can be kept occupied with a small haynet at which it can pick. However, it is sensible to use a small-mesh net, which will give the horse more to think about and will prevent the hay being eaten too quickly.

Once in a while there will be a strong-minded, wilful individual, a confirmed breaker of tie-ropes, whose behaviour will need to be countered by a short, sharp lesson. In days gone by such reprobates were fitted with a railway headcollar. (When the railway companies were much in the business of transporting horses, such heavy-duty, almost unbreakable, articles were in common usage.) A very strong rope was attached to this and the miscreant was tied up to a telegraph pole, often being encouraged in its attempts to break loose. What ensued was neither edifying nor humane. The poor horse fought until it was exhausted and when all its efforts to free itself had failed, it was deemed to be cured. Perhaps it was, but at what cost?

A more subtle, but infinitely more acceptable, piece of equipment was to fit **Galvayne's leading harness**, that simple device of soft cotton rope made to pass round the animal's quarters (or, if a more immediate effect was thought necessary, round the dock), while the two flank ropes, held in place by a support rope of similar material, were passed through the wall ring to the headcollar. The horse ran back but instead of the expected pull on the headcollar, it experienced a salutary and confusing pressure round its quarters (or dock) as the rope

A plate from Galvayne's book *The Horse* (1888) showing the leading harness being used on a persistent breaker of headcollars

tightened. The pressure was removed when the horse decided to move forward, a lesson few horses were slow to grasp.

The same principle is employed by fitting a thick, well-padded, soft-rope slip-knot round the horse's barrel. The rope end is then passed between the forelegs, through the headcollar and fastened to the tethering ring. When the horse runs back, the slip-knot tightens round its middle but again the expected pressure on the headcollar never materialises.

At this point, the watching trainer (for this little ploy must *never* be tried without keeping the horse under observation) steps in to relieve the discomfort by loosening the knot. The psychological effect is important: the horse associates running back with an unpleasant experience and the intervention of the trainer with relief from its self-imposed discomfort. ('Official' instruction is for the horse to be tied to a string loop that will break when the horse runs back. That avoids possible injury but it could be argued that because the horse frees itself easily it will continue to repeat the exercise. Use a string loop by all means, but keep the animal closely supervised as well.)

Biting and Kicking

Biting and kicking are parts of the horse's defence system, but they are secondary defences that are used seriously only when flight, the first line of defence, is made impracticable.

Both 'vices' are also concerned with aggression, which plays just as much a role in the make-up of the horse as in the human.

Biting and kicking are also symptomatic of uncertainty, confusion and irritation. They may frequently become evident in conditions of restraint when, for instance, the horse is tied up and becomes excessively anxious because of what may be a feeling approaching claustrophobia.

These failings, particularly kicking, seem to appear more frequently in mares than in geldings. A mare kicks at a stallion when she is not ready for mating, to show him his attentions are unwelcome, and she employs the same tactic to see off geldings who may be making a nuisance of themselves.

(Sometimes a mare may kick determinedly at her foal when it attempts to suckle, but more often than not this is because her teats have become sore and the suckling causes positive discomfort. This is one instance where sympathetic human intervention is usually able to cure the problem by alleviating the condition with udder salve or something similar.)

Because kicking by mares is a natural reaction to the overly impatient stallion and may therefore be reproduced just as naturally in company when at freedom, many establishments insist upon mares and geldings being put out in separate paddocks for grazing.

One of the most dangerous aspects of kicking occurs when a group of horses are fed in their field. Under these circumstances, horses easily become aggressive and excited as they compete for the food. There may be no intention on their part to hurt the bearer of the food but since he or she is the focal point, the situation is obviously a potentially dangerous one and should be treated accordingly. Clearly, it is inadvisable to feed one horse and give nothing to the others. If circumstances make this necessary, then some arrangement has to be made to remove the horse from the field before giving it the food.

If all the horses are to be fed, the ideal would be to put the feeds out in a separate enclosure before letting the horses through, but that, too, might be impractical in many instances. All in all, the feeding of, say, six horses in one field is fraught with danger for both horses and humans. When it cannot be avoided it should not be attempted single-handed, a competent helper being used to keep the horses off while a companion puts out the feeds. Incidentally, it is safer for everyone, and will help to prevent bullying if more feeds are put out than there are horses to be fed – eight feeds for six horses, for example, and spaced well apart.

Kicking in the Stable

In my experience, horses kick in the stable and at the attendant for three principal reasons:

1   The horse is ticklish and thin–skinned and the human is too heavy-handed, or employs brushes that are too scratchy. Very often well-bred chestnut horses come into this category, for their skin is usually more sensitive and the hair finer than that found in a grey horse, for example. The solution is to clean the ticklish parts, usually on the underside of the belly and between the hindlegs, by using the empty hand in a circular movement. At the same time, one should position oneself with care and close up to the horse, working from front to rear, or, when possible, using the free hand to exert at least a suggestion of restraint on the leg.

2   Heightened nervous reactions caused by high feeding and a state of peak fitness.
      Horses in this last condition are likely to lift a leg, or do worse, out of impatience, irritation or whatever and as the horse has been brought to this point as a result of a deliberate programme of training, feeding, etc., its behaviour is something that we have to accept while taking reasonable precautions against being hurt. (It is, of course, sensible to examine the diet in case there is an imbalance of energising food, when a change of rations and an increase in the fibre content may improve the situation.)
      The secret is first in working quietly, but none the less firmly and briskly, close up to the horse's body, and then in

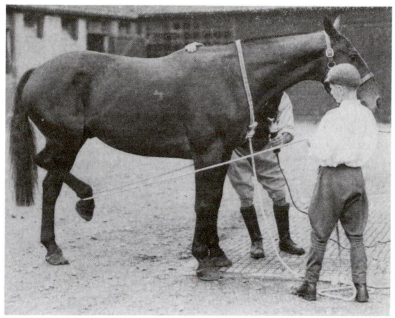

An effective way of dealing with a kicker whilst he is being clipped

resisting any tendency towards over-reaction should the horse forget its manners. If the handler starts to shout or perhaps to retaliate physically (which are, indeed, unmistakable signs of his or her nervousness), the horse instantly becomes more upset. It may become increasingly violent and a situation is created in which the horse may swiftly be reduced to a dangerous, hypernervous neurotic.

It is not unreasonable to check a horse when it gives notice of its intention to kick, which it does by a tensing of the muscles on the belly, but a restrained vocal reprimand, delivered without interrupting the grooming process, is far more effective than any other.

Nor is it unreasonable for fit horses to snap at their handlers either when being groomed or, which is even more usual, when being girthed up. However, a bite, whether it is looked upon as a reasonable reaction or not, is still painful and can, indeed, be incapacitating. The answer is to tie the horse up sufficiently short so that its teeth are quite unable to reach the target.

3 Horses kick, or threaten to do so, when they are anxious, uncertain of their handler and their surroundings or otherwise confused by the general environment.

Usually, in these instances, the horse turns to present its rear to anyone entering the stable – an understandable defensive posture, if somewhat disturbing.

The long-term solution lies in correcting the shortcomings of the environment, and it takes time, tact, talk, a few titbits and a lot of quiet confidence. It is also helpful with such horses to leave the headcollar in place.

Some horses, fortunately not many, may attempt to chase the intruder off their territory, i.e. the loose box, but most content themselves with defensive displays. In the first case, it is necessary to stand one's ground and, if possible, advance on the horse, attempting to get to its shoulder and thereafter to stay there. In the second, one has still to get to the shoulder, but our efforts should be concentrated on getting the horse to come to us rather than the other way round. It may take half an hour, sitting in the box and just talking quietly. In the end, the horse will give in and move over to satisfy its curiosity. Then it is rewarded and we must make much of it. It is not advisable at that point to saddle the horse up and take it out to work; it is far more sensible to give it a feed so that it begins to associate the human presence with pleasurable happenings.

Door-banging

Door-kicking is either due to impatience at feed times or to having been fed at irregular intervals. It can be symptomatic of boredom and general unease or it can become habitual because the horse has learnt that it attracts attention. As for the horse kicking the walls of the box, well, it could be equated with the prisoner knocking on the walls of his cell. Again, it is a question of providing an acceptable environment – a box where the horse can see and touch a companion over the partition, for instance.

A little intelligent management at feed-times (feed the impatient horse first) will reduce door-banging, but a bar placed strategically across the doorway, to prevent the horse hitting the door, is a useful deterrent and may save the horse from injuring itself, although it should not prevent it from looking out. Sometimes, padding the inside of the door is effective and, of course, it saves the risk of injury, but more often than not the horse goes on thumping, though less noisily. If the horse is otherwise reliable, a short chain hung across the open doorway is a solution.

Rug-eating

Horses are not unlike children – without plenty to occupy their minds they get into mischief, and some horses, like some children, will get into mischief anyway.

There is nothing more irritating, or expensive, than the confirmed rug-eater, and since it is impossible to oversee the animal every minute of the day and night, the final solution may be to take preventive measures of a mechanical nature.

Rock salt in the manger; a small-mesh haynet that prevents the hay being eaten up quickly; even some form of plaything hung in the box, can all help to reduce the incidence of rug-eating and, combined with good horse-management, may keep tearing propensities to acceptable limits.

There are those who advocate smearing the rug with some obnoxious substance but it is far too messy an operation to be recommended. Indeed, quite a few horses develop a taste for the stuff and continue their depredations with renewed vigour as a result.

Sometimes a change of stable-clothing does the trick. One horse of mine, with a genius for getting into trouble, would take a quilted rug to pieces overnight. Fitted with a plain, jute rug, he made no attempt to continue the game.

The one nearly sure remedy is to fit a **clothing bib** to the back of the headcollar so that it passes behind the lower jaw and extends below the muzzle. These are obtainable in leather,

A leather bib fastened to the rear of the headcollar is a deterrent against rug-tearing

which is expensive and likely to get spoiled by being immersed in water as the horse drinks, or in strong plastic, which is more satisfactory in every respect. Of course, its fitting involves the horse wearing a headcollar, at least throughout the night, but on balance that is preferable to the destruction of expensive clothing.

If the bib fails, the last resort is to use an **open-bar muzzle**, which will allow the horse to drink and to get at its hay but usually makes rug-nibbling too frustrating an exercise to be enjoyed and in which to persist.

Bandage tearing

Bandage-tearing usually occurs when horses are bandaged to protect an injury. Possibly the horse tries to remove the bandage because it is uncomfortable but, none the less, it is better if the dressing can be kept in place. A bran poultice on a foot is also often an irresistible and understandable temptation, but methods have to be found to prevent its removal.

A bib may be effective but a **neck cradle** is the only sure

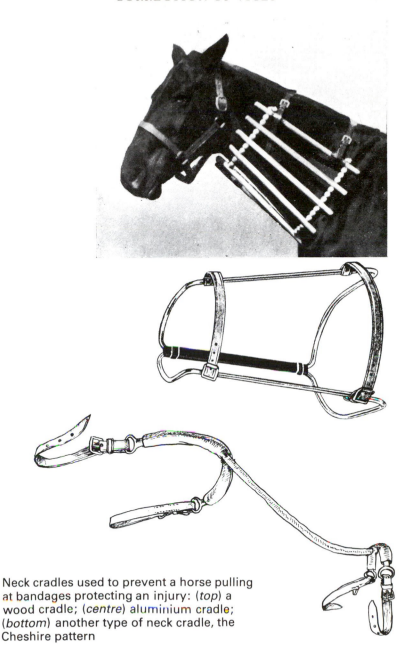

Neck cradles used to prevent a horse pulling at bandages protecting an injury: (*top*) a wood cradle; (*centre*) aluminium cradle; (*bottom*) another type of neck cradle, the Cheshire pattern

deterrent. The common pattern is made of separated lengths of turned wood linked with fastening straps. It works very well but it is very restrictive and it can chafe around the top end of the neck. A more humane device, which is less restrictive, is the **Cheshire pattern cradle**, or one can employ cross reins or ropes. These are attached to the side-rings of the headcollar, taken back to cross over the wither and then secured to a roller. They allow a degree of movement but not sufficient for the horse to get at the bandage or dressing.

Food-bolting

Feed-time brings its own problems, notably the horse that bolts its food in its anxiety to finish up the contents of the manger in record time, and second, the one that wastes its feed by thowing it from side to side and out of the feed receptacle.

In both instances, these frenetic performances suggest a stress situation caused by feelings of insecurity and/or, perhaps, a highly strung nature. That, however, might be too glib a solution and in any case is not very helpful. Both failings must be discouraged. Bolting food leads to digestive troubles, which can become serious, while food thrown on the floor fails to fulfil the purpose of nourishing the horse in full measure. The reasons for this sort of behaviour provide an interesting subject for discussion and conjecture, but in the end one has to employ practical counter-measures to eliminate the problem.

A few large smooth stones or, even better, some lumps of rock salt, put in with the feed, will compel the bolter of food to slow down and pick about for its rations. If the animal demolishes the contents of a haynet so voraciously as to induce indigestion, make use once more of a small-mesh net.

For the sweepers-out of food, use a corner manger fitted on each side with 'anti-waste' bars that will limit the sweeping movement of the head very effectively.

Tongue over the Bit

One of the more irritating equine problems is caused by the horse getting its tongue over the bit. To do so, it is necessary for the horse to draw the tongue backwards before laying it over the mouthpiece. The effect of the action is to reduce the extent of the rider's control to an alarming and possibly dangerous degree. In extreme instances, the tongue may be withdrawn so far back as to block the larynx, a condition described as 'swallowing' the tongue. When this happens, the horse comes to a sudden halt and, until the obstruction is removed, is in danger of choking.

If the horse is being ridden in a jointed snaffle, the first remedial measure to be taken is for this to be replaced with a mullen (half-moon) bit, the construction of which makes it more difficult for the horse to indulge in this particular resistance/evasion.

Indeed, if the bit is adjusted high enough in the mouth, this may be sufficient. If not, there are a whole range of items designed to frustrate this particular addiction. The first of these is the **Juba rubber tongue port**, which is fastened round the centre of the mouthpiece, the port or spatula facing the rear and lying flat on the tongue. Obviously, this device will encourage the horse to keep its tongue in the proper place.

A **tongue grid**, suspended by an independent headpiece above the bit, is something of a mouthful but it is without doubt another most effective deterrent to this unfortunate habit.

Racehorses that bring their tongues over the bit may be dissuaded by the use of a **tongue strap**, which encloses the

Both the rubber Juba port (*left*) and the tongue grid (*right*) will frustrate efforts to get the tongue over the bit

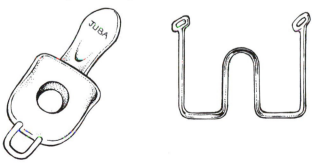

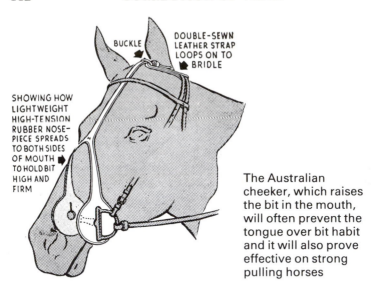

BUCKLE

DOUBLE-SEWN
LEATHER STRAP
LOOPS ON TO
BRIDLE

SHOWING HOW
LIGHTWEIGHT
HIGH-TENSION
RUBBER NOSE-
PIECE SPREADS
TO BOTH SIDES
OF MOUTH
TO HOLD BIT
HIGH AND
FIRM

The Australian
cheeker, which raises
the bit in the mouth,
will often prevent the
tongue over bit habit
and it will also prove
effective on strong
pulling horses

tongue and is fastened securely under the lower jaw. At best this is a Draconian solution and because of the discomfort it may cause it can only be used for a very short period of time. Outside of racing (and, perhaps, even within the sport) it is a barbaric device.

Far less distasteful and by no means ineffectual is the **Australian cheeker**. Made of rubber, the cheeker fits over the bit rings on either side, the central strap running up the face and being fastened to an attachment on the centre of the bridle's headpiece. It raises the bit in the mouth, while also allowing resilience on account of the material from which it is made. In itself, this removal of pressure on the tongue makes it much less likely for the tongue to be drawn back in an attempt to clamp it down over the mouthpiece. Furthermore, it acts as a remarkable restraint on a strong-pulling horse and is quite devoid of forceful persuasion. For no reason that is clearly understood, anything running up the centre of a horse's face exerts a form of psychological restraint.

14: Useful Oddments

A **lunge rein** has uses over and above the obvious one. A pair of lunge reins, attached one to each side of a trailer or horse-box and then crossed behind the horse, are excellent loading aids. (A yard-brush brought up resolutely behind a resisting horse and, if necessary, applied sharply to its back end, produces immediate forward movement and has also to be accounted as a valuable loading aid.)

A lunge rein can also be used to deal with those irritating equines who trot off just as one is about to catch them up in the field. Two people with a lunge rein can 'push' the animal into a corner where it can be more easily apprehended.

Horses that are difficult about being caught are best put out in a headcollar fitted with a 45-cm (18 in) rope lead attached to the back ring. (At one time such animals were hobbled. This worked, I think, but it is not much practised today.)

Mr Russel's foot leveller was once a near-statutory item in the

Mr Russel's invaluable foot leveller calibrated to show the exact slope of the foot

best-run establishments. This is a brass horseshoe fitted with a movable arm that is calibrated to show the slope of the dressed foot. In the forefeet the angle of the foot from the coronary band to the toe should approximate to 45–50 degrees and be virtually in line with the inclination of the shoulder from its point to the wither. When that angle occurs there is a foot-pastern-axis (FPA) that ensures the most economical flight path for the foot. The angle of the hindfeet is steeper, being between 55–60 degrees. (Some tact and diplomacy are required when introducing this useful item to the average farrier.)

Jowl and neck sweaters belonged to the show stable, where they may yet be in use. A jowl sweater is shaped like an attenuated pair of blinkers, with holes for the ears but not extending over the eyes. It is made from thick felt covered on the inside with oilskin or plastic and its purpose is to refine, by sweating, the over-fleshy jowls that sometimes occur in ponies and which make it difficult for them to flex at the poll. It was worn while the pony worked and the sweating it induced helped

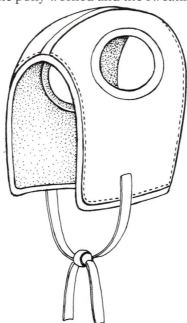

The jowl sweater helps to break down unwanted fatty tissue

to break down the fatty tissue. Neck sweaters worked in the same way to slim down thick and over-cresty necks.

On the same principle a body roller, similarly lined at the pads and belly, was put on ponies while working and even in the stable, in order to get rid of surplus fat and create something approaching a waistline.

A **sausage boot** is a soft, bulky ring strapped around the coronet to prevent capped elbows caused by the heel of the shoe bruising that area when the horse lies down.

The sausage boot is fitted round the coronet to prevent the heel of the shoe bruising the elbow when the horse lies down

Manes, by custom, lie on the off side of the horse's neck for the reason that it is usual to look at a horse from the near side, when the line of the neck will appear to better advantage if it is not broken by the mane. Some manes, however, refuse to conform to the considered norm. Such can be persuaded to do so by wetting them daily and attaching small weights to the ends. Otherwise, one can use a **mane layer**, two fairly heavy pieces of wood about 5 cm (2 in) wide that are fastened together with a butterfly nut at each end, with the mane sandwiched between them. A thick paste of flour and water plastered over the mane will also do the job well, but it is messy.

There are no aids for pulling a tail but it is wise to observe commonsense precautions in some instances. To pull the tail (little by little and certainly not all at once), it can be placed over the stable door, when the tail puller can operate in safety.

Strange but true. This is a
nose-net, a simple but
very effective remedy for
a puller. It will also, of
course, prevent the horse
from biting his
companions or, in the
instance of polo, his
opponents on the field

Otherwise, a bale of straw, hung round the neck of the handler while the tail is pulled, provides adequate protection against a kick.

A parting thought was provided by an old horse-dealer friend of mine whom I consulted on a number of points. He said: 'My 'osses don't 'ave no tricks – they work too bloomin' 'ard.'